GOD
IS

GOD
IS

OMER DAWSON

iUniverse LLC
Bloomington

GOD IS

iUniverse books may be ordered through booksellers or by contacting:

iUniverse LLC
1663 Liberty Drive
Bloomington, IN 47403
www.iuniverse.com
1-800-Authors (1-800-288-4677)

ISBN: 978-1-4759-9298-4 (sc)
ISBN: 978-1-4759-9299-1 (ebk)

Printed in the United States of America

iUniverse rev. date: 07/03/2013

INTRODUCTION

This is a book which makes it easy for the reader to understand how he fits into the universal scheme. You will experience the feeling of tuning in to the infinite knowledge of the universe. This is one way for you to experience the wonderful feeling of being close to that which you have known on this earth plane. This is made possible, because you have shown enough interest to read this book.

You have been able to be close to souls on this plane when you were able to see them, touch them, and to speak with them. You will be able to see it is possible to be even closer to those who have moved to another level of consciousness. This can be a feeling of closeness that you were never able to sense when you had a physical, geographical separation between you on this plane.

You will note that this book attempts to explain the difference between a soul with a physical body, and one without it. This is the total difference between the two existences. Life continues after the physical body has been laid aside. This life is one that continues to do the things that either were not accomplished here, or the things which will insure the further raising of the soul's consciousness to a higher level of attunement with the infinite.

This is all being made possible, because loving souls on other planes are doing their best to help the new arrivals adjust to this new existence, and to prepare them for the work that must be accomplished on that level. You will be made aware of the many levels of attainment by the souls on other levels. This is only because you may have difficulty comprehending those many levels which the souls need to experience. You will be able to understand many puzzling things which may have bothered you up to this time. Souls may advance on a higher plane, or they may regress for some time, before they are ready to advance. This is particularly true of souls who have had many emotional hangups on the physical plane.

I am only able to do this writing when I can leave the physical plane, by going within, and letting this material flow through my fingertips onto the paper in this form. You too, are able to do this, if you can become quiet, and begin to look within. This is an easy thing to do. You will not try to make it happen, but you can relax, and let the universal power flow through you, as this is being done.

Now, it is time to show you some of the secrets of the universe which help make this possible. First, you must feel close to God. This is an absolute must. It is the basic source of this energy which flows through you, making this possible. Next, you must realize that this power is only for good. This is important, as it must be for the greatest good to the whole universal scheme, as it unfolds before our very eyes.

This again, is one reason that you must develop a positive attitude toward your fellow man. This same attitude must be felt toward all energy, on all levels of existence. This encompasses all existence, whether it is animal, vegetable, or mineral. What a wonderful way to begin to understand all of this energy which surrounds you every moment on this level. God does not love one more than the other, but this very wonderful power is what unites all existence. You must realize, this is the most important thing for you to grasp. It is the binder for all existence.

You will now be able to enter into a new world of experience, which opens up new avenues of knowledge for your psyche to expand upon. Life will have a new meaning for you as you travel. Every moment of every day will become one which could be the beginning of a new existence for you. It is time for you to make this commitment which is necessary for you. This commitment enables you to reach out into the universe to communicate with levels of existence. This is important for you as you need to expand your consciousness so it will include all forms of life, and all levels of consciousness. This consciousness represents the many houses spoken of in the Bible. These houses are many, and varied, but must be understood before you can understand existence itself.

With this behind you, you are now ready to become one with all existence in this great adventure called life.

CHAPTER I

THE INTRODUCTION OF THE STUDENT TO THE REALMS OF THE MOST HIGH

You will now experience life as it should be. This chapter holds the key for you to an understanding of all existence as you perceive it, and as you cannot perceive it. Will you now place yourself in a quiet place, and relax every muscle in your body. Begin with the head, and relax the muscles on the top, then the eyes, then the tongue. Let this eliminate the tension in the head. You will wish to relax the neck and shoulders completely. Take a deep breath, and relax the upper arms, lower arms, then the hands and fingers. Feel the tension flow out through the arms, hands, and fingers. Relax the back and shoulder muscles, letting the tension move out of this area. You will relax the chest and stomach, then let the tension flow through the upper leg, then the lower leg, then let it all pour out through the toes. Take another deep breath, then relax completely, all over.

You will feel at peace with yourself. Let the mind become as a screen. Keep it blank until you have become completely relaxed. You will first visualize yourself as a small person who can look into the minute details of a leaf in your garden. See the rough texture of the leaf. Walk among the bristly hairs until you come upon a tear in this leaf, out of which the life-giving juices are flowing. You will now be able to enter this cellular tube, and flow along its channels. Follow this intricate network until you reach the broken stem, which is the source of life for this leaf. You may wish to continue through this stem, into the branch, down into the trunk to the roots where the vital energy enters this plant. Now you will want to flow back up this channel to the small leaf. Experience the warm sunlight striking the upper side, and feel the cool side where the chemical changes take place, and the life-giving oxygen is given off.

You will notice the life-giving juices are not too different from your own blood. The energies from the earth are absorbed into the roots, very much like the energy absorbed into your own stomach wall, to be sent to all parts of the body. You will be refreshed, when you feel your first sprinkle of rain on the leaves, or take a drink from the recently moistened ground. Torn, or broken branches and leaves will register pain with you. You will be happy if soothing music is played for you, or if you are fed at regular intervals. Do you have a master who loves you, bathes you, touches you? If you have these things present, you will be a happy plant during this life cycle. You might feel anchored with your roots firmly planted in the earth, but you still have mobility. The pollen from your blossoms may be transferred to neighboring trees by the bees, birds, and gentle breezes. Your seeds may be carried by animals, and breezes as well.

All this, should help you to have a keener understanding of the plant kingdom, in relation to your own kingdom. All this, you may say is far-fetched. Yes, it will take the imagination of a little child to experience these sensations. This is important, and you will develop a feeling of closeness with all plants, and the balance they afford for life on earth as we know it.

You may wish to take a trip through the mineral kingdom as well. It would be no more difficult than the trip through the plant. Experience all these wonderful things as an insect, or a pet in your home. The possibilities are endless, and you will begin to feel at one with all of God's creations on this earth.

CHAPTER II

WORKING AND LIVING IN THE REALM OF THE MOST HIGH

This chapter will be one which should raise your level of concentration to that of a higher plane. This is as it should be for your greatest good. We have all been placed on this earth to do a specific task. Your Father in Heaven, knows what this task is, and your higher-self also is aware of this. It is up to you, to find out what this task is.

This is necessary, before you will be able to know if you are on the right track. Your meditations, and quiet moments, are the moments when the small voice within will give you the direction you need. Listen, and you shall know the truth. Be still, and let the power of the Father flow into your consciousness. This inner strength will be all that is needed to carry many on a constructive path, directed toward the goals which have been laid out for you.

Remember, you must let the Father direct you, and must be the loving, willing soul who is willing to do the wishes of the hierarchy which are completely in harmony with God's plan for Universal Advancement of all Souls. Some of us have not reached

4

the heights others have achieved, but this is no reason why we cannot all strive to do God's bidding on the level where we can be most effective. You are all being blessed, as you continue working on your level.

You may now wish to know that level you are on at the present. This isn't as important to know, as what am I doing about advancing my soul to a higher level of consciousness. Life will not be too difficult to fathom, if you just keep your attention focused on the truth. This can only be achieved, if you have faith in yourself, as well as the universal law. You will see that it is easier to advance spiritually on the earth plane, than on other levels. You are in a position to do much from this plane to help those who have moved to other levels of consciousness. It isn't for you or me to judge those who obviously aren't on an equal level with us. This is a personal, individual thing with each soul involved. The important thing, is to help those on all levels of consciousness to grow, and advance spiritually as rapidly as possible.

You will now be able to develop avenues of communication between others on other levels of consciousness. Once this has been achieved, you should be able to explore the past and the future with the present. At this point in your development, you will feel all sense of time only as the present. All this relates only to the present. Why then, should we not enjoy every moment as we live it? You have now been able to forget the mistakes of yesterday, and are no longer uncertain of the future. Your concerns about time, other than the present, should be erased from your mind immediately. Realizing the inner power of the Father within, makes this all possible. Once this inner strength has been manifested, all goals, and levels of attainment are made possible in his name. Now that you have learned to go within for answers, you have also eased the tensions built up in a fast-moving society.

A sense of well-being and perfection, can only be felt when a spiritually oriented student can learn to completely relax the physical body in meditation. It is important to quiet the mind, and think only of the energy of the Father flowing through you. When this can be achieved, you will be nearing the cosmic relationship necessary for further advancement. Know that God is all there is, there is none other. Walk in this path, and you will advance spiritually, at a rapid pace. You are being blessed as you travel by the many angelic hosts that look after your welfare. This is good, as you are never alone. God is with you always, and this help is indispensable in your progressing on this plane. It is possible for you to achieve the goals set up before you entered this plane. Complete your task, and you have made souls on all levels advance beyond your wildest dreams. You are one with all, and all is one with you. This is as it should be. The universal plan has a small part for each of us, and it is up to us to follow this plan as well as we might. Your awareness of this cosmic law, is what must be developed, before you will be able to complete this work.

Your intuitive sense must be developed, before this can be an effective method of following direction given to you. This can be developed by following your hunches about everything. Take a guess at the correct time without looking at a clock. Listen, for the wee, small voice. This can be a method of tuning to the infinite instructions that are beamed your way. No one is left out. This is for everyone, if you only take the time to concentrate on this method, you will be able to develop this sense. You should practice in your meditation, being still, and listening for this small voice. This voice can come from your higher-self, or your soul, which has much information available. In a deeper meditation, you will contact a higher level of consciousness, which will be more reliable in the directions received. Place into your conscious mind, before you meditate, or go to sleep, the questions or material you wish information about. State when these answers will be coming to you, and you will be alert at this time for the small voice, or intuitive answer which will be coming to you. Always give thanks for these instructions you will be given. This is one of the easiest things to achieve if you have a sincere desire to serve your Father, in whatever capacity he may choose. This is not up to you to say, but it is yours to do, in a loving manner, in his name. Fully realize, your true employer is the Father within. You are his loving servant who wishes only to serve him. Do this, and you will truly be blessed.

Now is the time for you to ask yourself, "What am I to do in this life?" Do this, and you have begun to move up the path. Do this, and you will automatically change your level of consciousness. You will find you are a different person than you were moments before. This very seed thought has much power. The power of the Father works in wonderful ways, and you will begin to see this take action, and go to work in your behalf.

Now, that you have asked this question, you will want direction. You may go to many psychics, and learned men, who are tuned into this infinite source of knowledge, but, you will soon find that the answers have been with you all the time. Ask, and you shall receive. Your Father knows what your task is to be, so why look further. One can become mixed up with too much advice from all angles. You will be able to sit in meditation, and visualize on your movie screen the action you will take in doing your Father's work. Do not be concerned, about how this will all take place. Put this energy to work and it will be done. It sounds easy, or does it? It may mean that you must take some time out of your life, or it might take a little money for the beginning. These will be available for you when the time has come for this action. Some action may be needed this very moment, other parts of the plan will fit into the puzzle in a few days, weeks, or months.

It isn't good, that you should sit down and let God make the initial moves. You must ask, you must use the tools that will set this action in motion. We have the privilege of sitting still, and not growing spiritually, or we can dig in, and row our Father's boat, only asking that he shows us the way. Do these things, and you will be free. You will be earning a freedom that may have taken eons of time to reach. This is a time when miracles are happening every moment. These miracles will only increase as you gain your freedom.

You must be prepared for anything, when this decision has been made. You may need a strong physical body which means you may need to change your diet and get more exercise. You may need to take training, or further your education for the task ahead. The doors will be opened, when you are ready. The task for you may mean you must help people in need. You may be called upon for leadership and direction to help with world problems, whatever the course of action, you must be ready. Do these things in his name, and you shall truly be free.

This is just the beginning of many ways for you to serve. Serving, is our reason for existing on this plane. Take this away, and the soul has no reason for existing in the human body. Get into this rhythm of the universe, and you can be at one with the Father, and all that he has created for your enjoyment. What a wonderful way to travel, as you continue on this path. As you continue to move along, you will become aware of the many mansions, and the loving souls who dwell in these mansions. You may wish to look back into past lives to find answers which may add meaning to your existence at this point in time.

Your background, before this life, will give clues to hidden character traits that may have lain dormant up to the present in this life. Your task for this life, may tell you to be more forceful. If this is the case, you may have been a great leader among men before, and it would be much easier to utilize this trait from the past. This is important when you realize time is an invention created by man. In the universal realm, there is only the present, so these traits may be made manifest in the now.

We are ready to cover other facets of existence. This is one reason you have chosen to be here at this particular time. We all have different strengths to offer in working out the course of action needed to fulfill the universal plan. We don't wish to be martyrs, but we do need to feel we have been able to contribute to the fulfillment of this plan. You are being blessed, as you continue on this path, following this course of action. You may ask, why me, or why must I do this or that? It isn't up to you to question this action. It is yours to fulfill as well as you might. If you continue to surround yourself with light, you will be safe in following a course of action which has been opened for you. Know that the doors are being opened for you, and that you will be able to do your part in this plan. Keep the faith, and know that you are being guided by divine light.

Continue to give thanks for the loving directions which are received. Let your ego step aside, and the directions will continue to flow through you. Let every moment of your life, be a loving moment of grace. Once this transformation takes place, you will find those who come in contact with you will look upon you with an understanding of the Christ working within your inner consciousness. There is no need for you to try to impress, or show others of your spiritual growth, this is obvious. The inner light of the Father, will shine upon all those about you. They are being helped by your presence, and you are being blessed for your devotion to the truth.

CHAPTER III

THE POWER OF GOD
IN YOUR LIFE

Now is the time for you to understand the why of this tremendous energy. It is difficult for one to comprehend when we have been led to believe that the material world, created by man is all there is. Nothing, has ever been truly created by man. All creation must have the sanction of the Father. The very germ for these ideas used in creating physical, material objects, has been born of our Father's womb. This energy is all around and through you. It permeates all matter. It is the very essence which unites all matter, as we know it. Once you have begun to clearly understand all this, you can appreciate the fact that all mankind are truly one. We can disregard race, size, and physical characteristics, and see only the face of our Father, as we observe this as truth.

It will be a good idea for you to begin to understand how the physical body is dependent upon the energy forces around it. Take a deep breath, and exhale slowly. You will be able to sense the tremendous energy flowing throughout your body, as oxygen is carried to all cells of the body. Take a small mouthful of food into your mouth, hold it, and you will be able to feel the energy strengthening your body, as it is being swallowed. What a wonderful way to begin to sense this energy flowing through you.

It is time for you to become aware of material objects about you. You may try holding the hand of a loving friend. It will soon be obvious that you can feel this pulsating energy flowing through your hands. It is possible to have this sensation even if you aren't touching the other body, just having it in a close proximity. It is also possible, now to sense this energy when you are being blessed by another, a great distance away. Our energies are always intermingled with others, and it might seem to be confusing, except it is also possible to separate these energies. Sometimes, a negative sense might develop when meeting a new soul. This can be traced to a time in a previous life, when you may have had a negative experience together. This is good, as it shows you must work on this to clear it up once and for all. Do not let these negative forces continue.

You may wish to sense the feel of various materials next to your skin. Cotton, rayon, linen, silk, and wool will feel differently. Enjoy this beautiful sense, as the varied textures will give off different amounts of energy forces. Some will seem too warm, or cool, while others could irritate the skin, or feel slick and smooth. Enjoy the sense of touch, smell, and the vibrations connected with sound. With small insects, and animals, motion will be noticed. This expended energy creates motion and sound. The small particles of clay will seem to move, as they are shaped to create various plastic forms. This energy force permeates and unites all matter on the earth plane, Understand this, and you begin to understand your role in this cosmic universe. We could feel small and minute, like a drop of water, or we could feel we are a part of the large ocean. Whether we feel we are micro, or macro cosmic, in a sense, will make the difference between one who feels at one with all creation, or one who has chosen to separate himself from the source.

You are about to enter upon a new way of living and thinking. Your relationship with God is something that has evolved over a period of time, which consists of many lifetimes. We all have such a background, and this makes us unique, because there is much that we must learn as we advance on the path to spiritual maturity. God is always present, and this is difficult for some to understand. Some have been brought up with the idea that God is there, and they are here. This means that the two can never be one. Such a separation means that man has not developed as he should. It means that he must sense the fact that he is at one with the Father, who has made all life possible. You may ask, "Why is this possible?" It is possible, only because man has been able to think for himself. He has been able to make decisions which affect his life on this earth plane. Man can either feel at one with the Father, or continue with this separation. If this continues, he will not show the spiritual advancement he should in a particular life. He may even begin to regress, which isn't the desirable path to follow. Man also begins to feel that the material objects he enjoys are the creations of man, rather than realizing that God had created all that we enjoy.

It is time for man to begin to realize that he cannot grow without the unity that is inherently his divine right. This will not be a feeling achieved only on the Sabbath, but will be something he will experience every moment of every day in his life. Man's total existence will be filled with the glory that is his own birthright. This is truly the return of the prodigal son. Return, and you shall know the truth.

Can you imagine how this would affect man's relationship toward his fellow man? When you begin to see the Christ in all souls with whom you come in contact in your daily work, you will find others will react differently toward you. Where people were unfriendly before, they will begin to smile and greet you in a cheerful manner. What a blessing this would be in all our relationships with our fellow man. This is a power for the greatest good of all mankind. This, too, would mean that man would have no other idols, but would only see and worship the Father. We are worshipping other gods, when we show the fears that are prevalent in our lives. If we are afraid we might lose our jobs, lose our health, lose our close family relationships, we have been separated from the power that has placed us here. Some will worry about such negatives as earthquakes, famine, disease, and wars. Much energy is wasted on such worrying, rather than seeing the perfection of God's creation. Seeing this perfection in all that we experience, gives a loving, positive power for good wherever we might be. We will be helping the energies on all levels of consciousness bring about the perfection that has been created by the Father. It is time for us to look back, and see where we have erred in our thinking, then we can erase all this, and begin with our new life, looking only for the good, expecting the best, and knowing that God is working to fulfill our needs. We need not continue asking, for our Father knows our needs, wants, and desires. Keep tuned into the Infinite power, and you will automatically enjoy all these gifts that all men should enjoy. Give thanks for these wonderful blessings as you receive them, and you will be rewarded as only you can begin to realize.

Now, you may ask, "How does this affect me?" I have always tried to do the right thing. Maybe I have cheated someone. The mere fact that this enters your mind gives it power. This negative must be balanced with a loving, positive action which has helped your fellow man. You must then erase this negative action from your mind, wishing only the greatest good for the soul you may have hurt. Be on the alert for these negative thoughts, and continue dismissing them, until you have only room for loving, positive thoughts in your heart. Now, you are truly doing the work that the Father has placed you here to complete. How can one continue to grow spiritually, when these negatives continue to eat away at the very center of your being? Know, and you shall be happy. Know, and you will never feel lack. Know, and you are strong, and healthy so that you might be equal to the task before you. Do this, and you will truly be at one with the Father who has given you this life. If you feel you are working within the Universal Law, then you must not let anyone or anything hinder you from following the course of action set forth for you to accomplish.

Once you have been able to concentrate upon a definite goal which has been set up for you to achieve, you must see each segment of this action to its completion. The instructions, I will repeat, are given to some in a vocal sense in meditation, or your dreams may be able to set forth these goals. Intuitive hunches are good to develop, as they will tell you much. These goals have been given to you because you may need to achieve these goals as you move along the path. The goals may be such, so that you may utilize hidden talents gained in previous existences on earth. Psychics have been a big help to many who need to know what they must achieve, but I encourage you to go within to find these things for yourself. Do not look to others for your greatest good, but look only within for these answers. Only then, can you be certain of your true purpose for this life. Once you have begun to master the technique of relaxing, and looking within, you will be able to look back in time, or look ahead to see what you are about to do. This is easier for you if you realize that the past and the future are in the now, as far as universal time is concerned. Your loving teachers and guides, are constantly in touch with you. They will help you if you just go within for the answers. It must be remembered, that teachers and guides will also benefit if you are showing rapid spiritual growth. They too are growing as they are able to assist you. This interrelation of entities, exists throughout all the universe.

No man is an island unto himself, but is interdependent with all creation. How then, can man become separate from his God? It is possible for man to develop beyond his greatest dreams. God, working through man can and does all things. The largest building and the smallest scientific discovery have their roots in God's creation. You might say, "How does this affect me?" It is easy to feel separate from one's own creator, and yet this is impossible to some extent. God is all there is, yet man can be free to make his own decisions. This allows man to feel that all he has created, is truly of his own making, and thus, how easy it is to worship other Gods, or idols created by man. This is the beginning of separation by man for his true relationship with his Father. Blessed is the man who can be humble enough to give credit to his creator for all that he has done. Blessed is the man who is able to work in his name, without thinking of the monetary reward, but only how he can serve the Father in any capacity which seems proper. Do this, and you have begun to reach heights of which you never dreamed. These heights are for those who are ready to advance above the paths chosen by many of their friends. It is a path you must be willing to take, even if you are the only one on it at this time. Jesus was such a man. He was willing to be different. He was willing to make the sacrifice necessary to make this path visible to his fellow man. Before his time, this was only a path which was prophesied by men who were enlightened enough to see the truth. You are being blessed, merely by the fact that you are interested enough to read the message given on the pages of this book. It isn't often, when one is willing to take the time to settle down with a book, which gives a message of truth for all to understand.

We have been able to advance at a rapid pace in this century. This is made possible, because the timetable has been speeded up in order to prepare man for the return of the Christ. Much is being done to raise the consciousness of mankind, so he will be able to understand what is about to take place in the coming century. The marvels of this time will be difficult for the average layman to visualize. The enlightened man will be able to see what is about to take place. God's universal plan is being aided by those of this earth plane, who have been sent here to complete specific tasks assigned to them. The entities, and loving guides and teachers on higher planes, also have their specific tasks to complete. All levels of consciousness are working beautifully together, for the greatest good of the universe. This does not say of *mankind*, as you might wish; it specifically states, "for the greatest good of the *universe*." This all encompassing phrase includes all of God's creation. It puts man in his rightful place as part of the total scheme.

By now, you must begin to think that this is an attempt to put man down in the sight of the total picture, as we now perceive it. It doesn't limit the position that man fulfills in this plan. It does help clarify, however, the true perspective that should be man's position in the total scheme of things. Man does have the great responsibility of carrying out the physical aspect of God's plan for the earth. This is as it should be. We have a unique responsibility as those who have direct contact with the creative forces which rule the earth. How we use this force, is up to us to a great extent.

We are beginning to understand the grave responsibility placed upon us in this manner.

It must be understood, that our Father has so much confidence in us, that he has given us the right to make decisions which would surely affect the future for this earth. There are certain checks, which regulate the decisions made by mankind. Men who are in positions of leadership, have earned the right to these positions, by previous training through eons of time. They have specific goals to complete during this life, and are being drawn to souls who have worked with them before, as a team. The teachers and guides are constantly working with these souls, to help them in making decisions which will help with the fulfillment of this Universal plan. Man must never think he is alone. He has loving souls on all planes, who are working for the greatest good of all mankind. You may ask, "How can we fail in the successful completion of this plan?" This plan will be completed, but it will have pitfalls, as this plan is being evolved. By creating a greater awareness, we can minimize the effect of the periods when man has slipped in his spiritual development. It is up to all enlightened Christians to send beams of energy to those in power, which will give them the positive power which is needed to work out the plan. Groups of souls meditating and praying together for the greatest good of all mankind, will bring out the strength in the leadership which is sorely needed in these troubled times. With God's infinite power, all problems are being solved on the earth today.

We have been fortunate to have many great souls returning at this time. The tempo is building until the day of the returning Christ. We are being blessed merely by being alive at this time. We are all doing what we can to prepare the way for the Christ. This is as it should be.

The plan is being instituted, and all of the forces that are available, are being used. Many who are working in behalf of the return, are those who were here at the time of Jesus, two thousand years ago. What a privilege it is to be active at this time in behalf of the Father. We have been the chosen ones to prepare the way for the Christ. What an opportunity for those who feel this need to serve the Father. There are groups of souls collecting all over the world. An even larger number are unifying in the area where the Christ will appear. This is a location where mankind is now predominately evil. Those who have repented will be saved in his name. Those who haven't repented, will be surprised when the new Christ appears. Some will proclaim him as the Messiah, but others will claim to be the Christ, and this is the beginning of the anti-christ. This will be a period of turmoil, but all will smooth out, as the anti-christ is found to be a mere imposter. Much damage will be done but it is necessary to fulfill the prophecy.

CHAPTER IV

THE HUMAN WILL AND THE DIVINE PLAN

This is the beginning of a chapter in your life, when you will be able to be in tune with the Infinite on all levels of consciousness. There are also some of you who will be able to become at one with the Infinite. All this and more, are made possible by the Father. Accept this, and you have begun to grow in a wondrous way. This is the way of all men who are becoming enlightened. This is the path of the great souls who have traveled this path all along. What a blessing it must be, when you have reached a higher plateau. Every step up this path, is a step toward complete union with the Father. Know, and you shall be able to sense the presence of all great masters, who are working for your greatest good. This is as it should be, as you are a chosen one if you have decided to move up this path. Many souls are able to enter this plane, and exist, without making any effort to grow spiritually, while others, who have no greater advantages, will reach the heights. This man is truly blessed as he travels, and you are able to understand the full meaning of this, once you have begun to make the assent.

It is now time for you to look at yourself, and ask yourself if you have been shirking your duty, or have you earnestly been searching for the truth. If the later is true, then you have been able to know thy Father's will, and this is as it should be. All souls have been able to choose the time of their arrival on earth, and with whom they will be able to complete the tasks that have been laid out for them.

Events have been planned for you, in testing your ability to meet these challenges. There are certain things which must be accomplished, as you will have to make up for errors made in previous lifetimes. You may have things to work out with those who will be close to you. What a beautiful way to have this chance. You have many such chances in correcting the mistakes you have made in the past. It should be clear to you at this time, to see how easy it is for you to correct the mistakes of the past. Why then, would it be so difficult for you to give many chances to those who transgress against you? Once this is clear, you will be able to use this to help those who need your help in correcting those hangups, which are making their lives so difficult to cope with. It may be difficult for you to understand this law, but it is one which is important for you to understand, before it will be possible for you to move farther along this path.

Forgive those that transgress against you, and you will reap untold benefits. You will be blessed by perfect health, and you will be at ease among all of the souls you may contact in your daily travels. An abundance in all good things, will be forthcoming with this change of attitude. Many have been so used to taking their frustrations out on others, they will find it difficult to accept this. To completely forgive, means that you have healed all wounds that may have been in the making for eons of time. Those of us, who still hold a grudge against another, who has moved to other levels of consciousness, on other planes have only to realize that it only hurts ourselves. The soul who has been freed, will not receive the negative vibrations sent out by the living entity. This soul, who is the intended one, will, in turn, be working wholeheartedly in behalf of the living entity. How foolish to be caught up in this situation, where a loving soul, who wishes only the greatest good for you, one who is working diligently in your behalf, could be the target for your hatred. Universal Law, works only for the soul who has learned to forgive completely. You can never be free, if this cannot be overcome. Blessed is he that is in love with the whole universe. Blessed is he, that is in tune with the whole Universal scheme of things.

You are now beginning to glimpse what is in store for you, when you let go and let God do all things. Life can be a beautiful experience, or you can make it a living hell. Live within the Universal Law, and you have achieved a sense of Grace, that will emanate from every atom of your being. You are the one, who can and will make your life what it is to be. Why would you wish to make a living hell of your life, when the loving Father wishes only the greatest good for you. Separate yourself, and you will never move along the path, but will only stagnate, or possibly regress in your progress. This message was given to us by the Christ, almost 2000 years ago, yet we fail to see the light. Since the Father has placed each and every one of us on this plane in this time, we must realize the divinity of every man we meet on our path. This is such a simple principle, that it is difficult to see why mankind will not accept this precept without reservation.

We shall now see why you will need to make this change in your life. How long have you been able to hold a grudge? Was it just fear, that instilled this in your consciousness? If fear was the motivating factor, then you must understand why this fear was allowed to creep into your thinking. This fear could have been brewing for eons of time, and it was allowed to fester, until it came into a level of misunderstanding that would be difficult to eradicate. Once this has been resolved completely, you have been able to change the vibrations from those of a negative force, into a loving, positive force for good. If this healing is complete, you will have no fear of this ever coming back to haunt you. It is only when you think you have corrected your thinking, but have reservations, that you will find these negative forces plaguing you. Be free, and forgive completely. The love of the Father flowing through you for this greatest good, makes these corrections possible.

Life all around you has been able to exist, only because it exists in a harmonious relationship with the environment which surrounds it. All this has been made possible, because the living, loving molecules existing in a magnetic field with other loving molecules, have been able to cooperate with the energies emanating from those other forms of matter. It might be; man, plants, animals, minerals, and liquids or gases that make up the universe. These forms, might give off heat and light, as the molecules continue vibrating at various rates of speed. If this is true, then it must also be true that man must be in harmony with his maker. This is something that must gradually take more and more of the time of the soul, as he remains on this plane.

This is a great time for man to develop at a faster pace than could be imagined. Souls are growing, and developing on all planes of existence, but here, it is possible to develop spiritual awareness at a rapid pace. This is possible, because the teachers, guides, angels, and living souls on other planes, are all working in your behalf. How then, can anyone say he is alone in this world? You are never alone. All of the forces of the Father, are being brought to bear in your behalf. This is the only way for man to travel.

Mankind must be able to remain tuned in, as these forces continue to act, and react about him. You must realize that it is as easy as sitting down and relaxing the whole body. Every muscle, and nerve must be completely at ease, before one is able to fully realize his oneness with the Father within. What a blessing this can be when this state has been achieved. What a joyous feeling will come over one, when this happens. You will never know what this can mean, until it takes place. The angels and loving souls will hover around you, as you begin to experience this feeling of ecstasy. Rejoice, and know that you have experienced a change in consciousness. You will never again be the same person you were moments before. This graduation is one means of moving to higher and higher levels of spiritual thinking, as you will travel up the path, leading to the culmination of many, many lives on numerous planes, and levels of consciousness. You are the product of those many lives on this plane, Each one has added something to your character which has helped fulfill your desires, and necessitated your return many times, until all has been accomplished. The Akashic records have kept a running account of your progress throughout all eternity. You have only yourself to answer to. You alone, must pay the price for failing to heed the commandment of the Father.

Now, is the time to make a decision to completely change your life. Now, is the time to renew yourself for the task ahead. Now, is the time for you to dedicate yourself to the Christ, in his name. Do this, and you will be eternally blessed as you travel. May the Father be with you, as you continue along this path, walking arm-in-arm with those who would help you along the way.

CHAPTER V

THE UNIVERSAL LAW AND ITS EFFECT UPON MANKIND

You are now able to understand much more than you did in the beginning of this book. It is necessary for you to begin at some point of departure, and then you will have a better idea, about where you are to go from that point. We have seen how man has been able to adjust to his environment; now, you will be able to see how the Universal Law affects man as he travels along the path to complete freedom. This has been an experience for you which helped formulate your thinking on higher and higher levels. Keeping yourself tuned into this power, will undoubtedly raise your level of consciousness to a higher and higher degree. It will be obvious to those about you when this begins to take place. Your light will shine out upon the world in a new and wonderous way. This light is a beacon for those who are in need of your help. The help you give to your fellowman, is repaid many times over. The more you give in his name, the more you receive in his name. This may be in the form of greater understanding, or better health. It might be that you will receive the blessing of the multitudes, as you travel. Whatever the case may be, you will benefit in his name.

The "I Am," is important for you to understand. To be in harmony with Universal Law, means that you must realize the source of your energy, and power. Realizing this, you will be able to do all things. You will be able to overcome all obstacles which might plague your life. The mere fact that this book is being written, is a function of Universal Law. This Law, can be interpreted in many ways, yet the basic Law as set down in the Bible, has made it very clear to us that it may be difficult to follow to the letter, but you will be able to find that it isn't so difficult, when you relax, and let God. Man's ego is his downfall. This is the reason he has made so many mistakes in the past. All you must do at this time, is to realize this power for good working through you. It sounds easy, doesn't it, but this is only the beginning.

You, as a physical being, must step aside, and let the Father guide you along the path. You must be a loving servant for the fulfillment of God's plan for the earth at this time. You might say, "Wow, this is more than I can handle." Yes it is, but you must be equal to the challenge. Do this, and you have become a loving follower of the Father; realizing, full-well that all that you are able to accomplish, can only be done when you let this power flow you. This doesn't mean that you are unimportant; it does mean that you understand the proper relationship between the Father, and yourself. Reach this level of thinking, and you have begun to realize full well, the very reason you have chosen to return at this time and place. You will begin to understand why certain doors have been opened for you. Those doors will not open, until you are ready to accept the truth hidden behind those doors. Believe, and you shall know. This is only one of many ways you will be able to gain this understanding. It is a very basic way, and for this reason, you must understand this first, before you are ready to advance to a higher level of consciousness.

Why not relax, and know that you are of the Father. Do this, and you will never be the same person you were minutes before. Do this, and you will never again, care what your fellow-man thinks of you. You will not ever have to think that you are better than others, but will be able to see that all mankind is of the Father. With this perspective, you can never feel that you can judge your fellowman, and that he has no right to judge you. In either case, you have grown instantly, from a simple soul to one that has gained in stature. One that has begun to climb at a rapid pace on this plane. If you are of the Father, then why not bless all that you will encounter in your loving environment. It will be easy for you to bless, and give thanks for all that surrounds you. How could you be an unhappy soul, when this understanding has been achieved? How could you go back to being that unhappy soul you were yesterday? You can't, and this is the reason it should be easier for you to advance, when you have received this understanding.

Now, you'll probable ask, "Why couldn't I understand this before?" You may have read many books, attended many lectures, and still never fully grasped the meaning of being at one with the Father. Man has the choice of how he thinks, and acts. This very freedom, can lead him to complete freedom, or to complete domination by the negatives he has allowed to build up in his thinking and actions. Your Father wants you to have the full, rich freedom, which you rightly deserve, and you can either accept this completely, or reject it completely. "Why would man be so stupid, as to take the later path?" Anyone in their right mind isn't going to follow the negative route, but millions of souls today, know of no other approach to living. Reverse the letters in the word live, and you have evil. The evil in your life, is the many compounded negatives that build up in your lives. This decision is yours, why not choose the path for a loving, harmonious union with Universal Law, set up by the Father. This is his wish for you, why not make it come to pass in your life, since you are of the Father.

It is time for you to understand why the Law is important to you, and to the world. This Law works from the smallest particle of life, to the largest accumulation of energy in any mass in the universe. Without this Law, you will have chaos. With this Law, you have Divine order, as it was meant to be. This disorder, can range from wars, or conflict between souls on this plane, or it might mean that it will show up as dis-ease, as the cells of organisms are confused or lost. Natural elements can bring destruction, when the negative vibrations are strong enough in a given area. Our Father, has his plan for you, as well as a plan for the universal scheme. Step out of line, and the negative vibrations will be felt. Being in tune with the Father, every moment of every day, helps keep this attunement, which is so important. Needless to say, there would be no wars, no disease, no disharmony, no lack for anything, if all mankind followed the simple precept of being at one with the Father. Much energy is being directed through each of us, by all levels of consciousness. We are all being guided, and helped to make the right decisions which follow the basic Law. Our physical bodies may resist this commandment, but the inner-self is always being guided by those on other planes. With all this help, you may ask, "why is it possible for one to disregard the Universal Law?" Man's strong will, is all that lets him make the wrong decisions. This is a proving ground for mankind, and each mistake, is a learning experience for him. Unfortunately, some just never seem to learn from these experiences. Thank the Father, that we are given so many chances to learn these lessons.

Let us assume that all mankind is about to live by the rules set down in Universal Law. This would mean, that the whole economy would have to be adjusted, to take up the slack in the work force. This would mean there would be no one to enforce the Law, as it would be obeyed in a loving manner. There would be no one to treat patients for numerous diseases, as mankind would no longer have any excuse to bring this on himself. There would be a few karmic hangovers, which would need attention during the duration of this life, but they would be able to return again with a sense of complete freedom. This freedom, can only be achieved when man had united completely with his Father which has made him. So far, man, by and large, has chosen to reject this freedom, but little by little the truth is beginning to seep into his consciousness. We are entering an age of enlightenment, which will herald the coming of the new Christ. What a joy it is, to be here on this plane, in this time of renewal. Each, has his appointed task to accomplish. It is up to each one, to understand, and fulfill this purpose as the need arises. The most difficult thing for us to learn, in this period of time, is patience. This is a word we have forgotten in the twentieth century. It is a word, which prepares us for the spaced-out sequence of events which will take place during the coming years, which will fulfill the prophecy as we know it. More and more people are becoming aware, and this helps make the good win over the evil negative prophecies which have been proclaimed by those who look to see the darkest side of things. Let us rejoice, and see the beauty and glory of the return of the living Christ. What a blessing this must be, from a Father who loves each of us dearly.

In this new age, we must look within for our answers. Those, who will do this, will rule the world. Do not look to your brother, for the answers to your questions, but go within to the Father, who will never forsake you. This union of your mind with the consciousness of the Father, truly makes you one with the Creator who has placed you on this plane at this time. "What is your purpose on this earth, this lifetime?" You ask. No one knows better than you do, what your reasons must be. Look back, and you can see a pattern unfolding for your life. Sometimes, the formative years, are only a preparation for the later years, when much will be accomplished. The learned patriarchs, and elders, have been known to be the wisemen of the culture in which they have been placed. Other wisemen, will be the young, who have learned much from previous lives, and have retained this vast storehouse of knowledge, to contribute to our culture. The greatest of these, however, must be the sage, who looks within, for his answers. He, can set himself aside, and let the knowledge flow through him, which has been learned throughout all space and time. This, truly is the level we must strive to achieve, if we are to really help our fellowman.

Man's dreams, have much which can be interpreted, and help define the real reason for being on the earth at this time. You are the best judge, of the interpretation of these dreams. Learn what the basic dream symbols are, and use them to help in the interpretation. The quiet moments of meditation, are best for finding the real reason for your being here at this time. In this period of quiet, you might hear a small voice, or see it in a visual, colored picture. You may go to sleep with the understanding, that upon awakening, you will be able to have the answers to those questions you might ask. Our teachers, and guides, are working in our behalf, to give us this knowledge if we are ready for it. Your higher-self, your soul, has recorded all of your past experiences. One who would use this knowledge foolishly, will not be able to receive it. We are only able to advance along the path, as far as we are able to understand, and use the Law wisely. Do not be impatient, if it doesn't come to you overnight. You must realize, that you will only receive, as you are ready to use it correctly.

Learn to live with the Universal Law, and you will inherit the earth. This literally means, that wonderful changes will take place in your life. Others, will look upon you, as one who is lucky, or can manifest miracles. You will be surprised when you have reached a new level of consciousness. This will mean that you will never be the same person you were before. You will learn to live with this new concept, and flourish with an abundance never before dreamed of. All souls who make contact with you, will go away renewed, and revitalized, with new hope of the good things to come into their lives. This is truly the way God has meant for us to travel along the path.

We are the ones, who throw up many roadblocks in our path; why not accept the truth, and live life to the fullest. This alone, must be a miracle, which surpasses all others. You have begun to accept much of the truth when you have reached this section of the book. Much more will follow in succeeding chapters. These are presented to you in a manner, which will begin to build one block of truth on another. There is so much to cover, that it is difficult to keep from giving all the truths in one feld-swoop. This material is meant only for the souls, who have reached a high enough consciousness, to understand the truths given herein.

Now you are going to visualize the whole concept of the truth, as it is offered. Man will never know how he could have existed before these truths became known. It is true, that man has not been able to exist in a harmonious way, nor has he been able to enjoy the gifts of the Father, as he should. The time has come, for all this to change. This is only one of many outlets, being used today to bring the truth to mankind. The Masters, teachers, and guides, are all working in behalf of all mankind on the earth today. The harmonious use of Universal Law, is important for the future of mankind. Each of us must do his bit, to bring about a perfect climate for the return of the Christ. We must be aware of our responsibility, in doing our part in this scheme. Your part, added to that of countless millions, will make an invinceable army for good on the earth plane. Those vibrations, felt at this time, will lift the souls of this earth to that of the angels.

The potential, is unlimited. The good, that is about to be unleashed upon the earth, will be recorded in the history of this era. Man, will not be known for his scientific achievements, but for his spiritual growth. This growth, will be on such a vast scale, that it isn't humanly possible for mortal man to comprehend. For once, all levels of consciousness will be united with the Father. This union, is something that has taken eons of time to bring about. Mankind, is about ready for this step. Much, must be done before this can come about. It is in the hands of the Father, and the timetable also is in his hands. It is up to us, to help with the proper method of carrying out this mission. The heavens will open up, and rejoice, when this event takes place. All mankind, will be at one with the Father, and this is good. All mankind will be tuned in to the Universal consciousness, and this is good. Mankind will now enjoy the efforts that have been put forth by the many countless souls, who have given their time and effort in this great cause. All, will benefit. All will be made better for it. All will be done in his name from that day forward. No man, will need to build his ego, as there will be only one ego, that of the Father.

You may ask, "how then, will man be able to exist?" Actually, man does not exist at the present, compared to the existence he will enjoy at that time. True, there will be no need for law enforcement agencies. The laws will lovingly be obeyed. There will be no hospitals, as mankind will be perfect, by accepting the perfection that is his. There will be no lawmakers, as there will be no one to break those laws. Man will be intuitive, and will instinctively know the thought patterns others may have, and be ready to work with others in a completely harmonious situation. There will be no need to have secrets from each other, but all will be tuned into the truth. This is all we need to know. It will be our pleasure to grow and harvest the foodstuffs. All facets of productivity for the good of mankind, will be lovingly accomplished. All will be accomplished easily, and with much less effort than it takes today. A natural system of distribution, will be used, which means all areas will be self-sufficient. There will be no lack, nor wanting for anything, as it will be the Father's good pleasure to provide this for us. Thank you Father!

CHAPTER VI

THE WORKING OF TRUTH IN CREATING THE BEST OF THE EARTH PLANE

Truth is such, as we may have many different interpretations of the meaning. The truth of the Father, is one thing, and the truth of man's relationship with his fellowman, is another. The truth we are to speak of, is on a higher level of consciousness. This means, that man is not ready for the truth, when he still holds back in his devotion of the Father within. This must be uppermost in his mind, as he begins to travel the path.

This truth, then, can set you free. It is the stuff, that makes for a sound structure. This is the only structure the Father would have us build. Truth affects even the smallest cell, and can shake a galaxy. The truth of the Father, means that you have united completely with him, with no reservations whatsoever. This is a simple but effective way of describing the truth, as seen from higher levels of consciousness. This is a truth that has not been veiled in any way, but is exposed as it should be for all to view. Will you now just sit, and listen for the truth to sink in. Be still, and know that this is so. Feel, that you are at one with the Father. Know, that nothing can sever the cord between you. Know this, and you are free. Know this, and you will be a soul among souls; a man among men. Know this, and you will feel the oneness of all creativity with the Father.

This creativity, is one that you will see differently. You can now observe, and realize that all creativity has been from the Father. All that we have, and all that we enjoy, are the creations of the Father. The first spark of an idea in a man's head, was not his own ego, but a part of God's plan, manifest through man. Why then, should man continue to say, "I did this, or I did that?" This is the wrong conception, as it stands, but you may say the same thing again, with the emphasis of the "I," as the Father within. Now, you have a different picture. Now, the truth will out. What a wonderful thought, when you can realize, that the "I," does it all. "Where does this leave me?" You might ask. Yes, you can say "I am nothing, or I am a part of the whole scheme." Certainly, you are nothing, when you have separated yourself from the Father. Certainly, it must be wonderful to feel you are a part of the whole universal scheme of things. Being a partner with the Father, is all there is. He guides, opens doors, and you, lovingly, will serve him in his name.

Certainly, you will wonder if this means you must live the life of a priest, or some type of religious nut. This means, only that you have dedicated yourself to serving God, through the Christ. It means, that you will be a normal individual, who is working in behalf of the Father. It makes no difference, how much money you have, or what vocation you follow. It does mean, that you have dedicated yourself to serving the Father. With this in mind, how could all the common sins of today, be at work in your life. Such words as; envy, greed, jealousy, hatred, fear, and resentment, could all be dropped from our vocabulary completely. These words will automatically be replaced by; love, compassion, grace, wisdom, mercy, and understanding. Set yourself on a course like this, and you will have eliminated all negatives from your life; not because you have tried hard to forget them, but because you have accepted the truth. You will have time only for loving, positive thoughts, and will have no fear of the negatives returning.

Let us now perceive what it would be like, if man would never think of the creator, or would never give thanks for the many blessings which have been bestowed upon him. All this has been made possible by the goodness of the Father. It is his work and plans, which make this possible. We are being blessed every moment we are on this plane. We are being loved, and blessed every moment on all levels of existence. This makes it possible for man to feel secure in the fact that he is never alone, but is being helped in every aspect of his daily life. You can never know, what this could mean to countless numbers of beautiful souls. This is exactly what many need when they are alone. It is what people need when they are in need. We should never feel we are fighting the battle alone, but that we have the help of countless numbers of guides and angels. These loving entities are always with us. They will work in our behalf, even when we are not aware of such help. This is what is needed in order for us to accomplish many things which seem to be impossible. It is the help we need to open the doors, which gives us the direction we so dearly need. Will you now just relax, and give thanks for this help in your life. It is possible for you to look back upon your life, and see how many of the so-called miracles which have happened in your life, were all part of a divine plan.

Why not enjoy this life, and let it happen as it will. All you must do is, be prepared to go through the open door when it is opened to you. Be ready for any eventuality, for it might come tomorrow, or next year, but it will come. You will be able to know what the divine plan has for you. This can only be so, when you are receptive to the intuitive hints which will bombard your consciousness. What an instrument for good you will become. This instrument will be used only for the work the Father has outlined for it. The least you can do, is prepare yourself, by keeping your physical body trim, and in good order. You will need plenty of sleep, good wholesome food, and to associate with those who will be of benefit to your greatest spiritual unfoldment. With this in mind, you will be invincible. You will be one who has inherited the earth. None can harm you as you travel. Divine love shall protect you, with no reason to fear anyone, or anything. There is no power, but that of the Father, so why worry about failure, or have any doubt about the success of the work that has been set before you.

It is now possible for you to take advantage of the situation, selfishly, and make use of this power, as you have begun to understand it. Do this, and you will be paying dearly for it for an eternity. Live by the truth, and you shall succeed in all that you will set out to accomplish. Do this in his name, and you have the blessings of the universe; do this, and you will be invincible. How can you fail, when you have the full cooperation, and backing of the Father, in all that you will do. All that you do is being done with the divine plan in mind. This should be one of the greatest moments of your life, when you have begun to understand, and use this law, as it was meant to be used. You are one who will be greatly enhanced, when this spiritual unfoldment begins to take place. Those about you will know this is so, and you will have to tell no man, for it is known before you travel this path. None can fail to recognize the truth, when they see it. Others will see the face of the Christ in your countenance, when you pass. Just living, and being the spiritual one you are, is all that is required in the beginning. The dedication, and work, must follow this, before you can be as effective as you will need to be.

One, who has received the truth, will never need to prove this fact. If you have received the truth, you will never be the same person you were moments before, as you will have been raised in consciousness, to a level, higher than reached before this time. Once you have begun this steady rise, as you progress along the spiritual path, you must never digress, lest you will have to pay the price, of one who has failed to keep the commandments. What a blessing it is, to keep this commandment. It is our sacred trust, and we must do what we can to see that this truth must continue in our progress. No, God will not strike you down, you will have struck yourself down, by not following the path set forth for your life. You have begun to see that the path of righteousness, is a divine plan, one that has been set, long before you were placed on this earth. This has been one that knows no past, no future, only the now. This very moment is the most precious moment of your life. Know this, and you shall begin to get the full meaning of the now, in your life. Without this now, there could be no past, or future. What spiritual unfoldment that takes place at this moment, determines what progress you will begin to show. This is the greatest of all moments, when you have begun to grasp the full meaning of the present, and what it can mean to you. The whole universe, is dependent upon this moment, to make the whole thing function properly. Why not become part of this total picture, and enjoy the blessings of the present.

Beyond this, there is much which we have not begun to discover. The secrets of the universe, need not be secrets any longer. As this begins to unfold, before your very eyes, you will begin to understand, why you have had many problems in the past, or why you didn't wish to do certain things, when they should have been accomplished. Many everyday occurrences seem to just happen, but you will find, that it all has been programmed and is being acted out, according to a definite plan. This, is what we must begin to understand, and this is the reason, we are here at this time, and place. Nothing is left to chance, but our Father is the one we must ultimately give the credit for this miracle of all miracles. There are many sub-chiefs, and many guides, and teachers, who are involved, as well as many enlightened souls, who are working in our behalf. You have been fortunate to have discovered this. We have all been ready to accept material like this many times, but for one reason, or another, we have been afraid to accept the truth, when we see it. We have been trained, to believe what we can see, and can recognize with the other senses we have available; but the sense of perception can be quickened to see and understand much more than we were able to before this time. You are beginning to explore the unknown, and it will make sense to you when it has been revealed to you. This unknown is something which has been known, and understood for eons of time, by many souls, who were ready to accept this knowledge. You, must also be ready, or you wouldn't be here, looking at this page. The next Chapter is one which will begin to outline some of the material which should help the sincere searcher for the truth.

CHAPTER VII

YOU WILL BE SAVED ONLY WHEN YOU KNOW THE TRUTH

You must have been waiting for this moment, the moment, when you can begin to open the door a crack, and let a little light enter your consciousness. Much has been said of the truth, but here we are concerned with, how does this truth affect me? What do I get out of this? This is understandable, but it must first be in your heart to be willing to see the light, and let this flood your very soul, to the everlasting joy of the angels, who watch over you. This is the largest, single step you must take, in this upward movement of your inner-self.

The truth, is clearly spelled out, in the teachings of the Christ. It is up to us, to interpret these, and make them work in our daily lives. The teachings are very simple. The Mosaic Law, was the first, but Christ made it more meaningful for us. Moses considered the law, to be strictly enforced on the action of the doer, but Christ has added another dimension, which included thinking about doing the action. Its just that simple. We now have a glimpse of the truth in action. Every thought wave you send out, has power, whether for good or evil. Why not make those thoughts for good? Evil, negative thoughts, can only bring harm to you, when you use them. Loving, positive thoughts on the contrary, can only bring good into your life. This good will be, health, abundance, happiness, and many other positive traits. The contrary is true, when the reverse goes into action.

Sickness, disease, financial misfortune, loneliness, and despair, would be your lot, if the negative forces were to take over completely. You can say, "This is the work of the Devil," but I say to you, that this is of your own making. You can make your own heaven or hell, on this earth. Usually you will find, that the average soul, will be living a mixed up life, using both the positive and negative attributes, as he moves along during the course of a day. Some days, we will tend more toward one, than the other, and at other times, the reverse is true.

Will you now just relax, and take a breath. In due time, you will find it will be easier for you to live a happy, positive life. A life, that will work smoothly, and one which will give you sufficient time to devote to your spiritual growth. This is the real reason you should make this change, if for no other reason. All this will be possible, as you will have sufficient energy for this task, and your mind will not be burdened with the worries of the day. Meditation, cannot work successfully for you, if you cannot relax completely. A loving, happy soul, can and should do this regularly. Meditation will come easier as you travel up this path. It will become so spontaneous, that you may not be aware of your meditating at all. This can, in some instances, become your way of life. It will happen at your work, and during the hours of leisure. Formal times should be set aside for this purpose, but informal meditation should take up much of your time.

What a way, to remain tuned in to the cosmic ethers, which surround us. How is this all going to help mankind? This is a common question, when one is asked to do something which will take some of his precious time. First, your being tuned in, will effect all those, with whom you will come in contact during the day. They will be blessed, for having made this contact with a loving soul. None of those people, can walk away, and be the same person they were moments before. This is easier understood, when you realize that we are all in a constant state of change. Nothing, remains constant, in the universe, but is in a constant state of change. All of the beautiful souls who come in contact with you, have changed, and will go out, and create a loving, positive change in the souls they will meet. What a power for good, can stem from one loving soul. Look at the effect Christ had on his disciples, then see the effect they had on mankind for two thousand years. True, the truth was twisted, many times, and it will be corrected, but it still had a fantastic amount of energy generated from one man. Think, what would happen, if this truth remained unadulterated?

God willing, we will see a universe, where all souls will live together in loving harmony, with no power given to material things, and spiritual growth is all important. All material developments, will be attributed to our Father, who has made this all possible. The scientist, and the theologian, will be of one mind. We will be able to see, that all mankind has one mind, and that mind is in tune with the whole universe.

Will you now do something which will startle the world? Will you dedicate yourself to serving the power that has placed you here on this earth, at this time? This dedication, is important for mankind, as well as for the growth of your spiritual self. It is time for all mankind, to rededicate himself to serving all mankind, in any capacity which will be suitable at the time. Who are you, to question what, or how you should serve the Father?

The important thing for you, will be to make the most of every moment, which has been given to you.

Know this, and you will be a leader among men. You will be given the scepter, which designates the level of your work. This is such an important task, that one link be broken, or weakened, and the universe will suffer. You are important, as you will never know. Each link of the chain for eternal life, must be securely forged. It must be created, so it can be a help to all mankind. With everyone doing his prescribed task, the universal plan will be put into an effective method of sharing the burden. Each of us, has a grave responsibility to do what is asked of us, in this life. Ask, and you shall know what your prescribed task will be. Learn to concentrate, and focus your attention only on the truth, and nothing will deter you in your progress, at this time. How great it is to see one who has reached this inner state of bliss. How many of you will ever know, the true meaning of the truth, as it relates to your being saved, in the eyes of the Father?

The mere fact that you have shown an interest in this material, will show that you are on the path, at a specific point in time. Time, as related to the eternal universe, is not the same as the time that man has created, for his convenience. We all, are on the path, but on different levels of understanding. Why then, should man be critical of his fellow man, when he is on a different level of understanding? This is a personal thing with each of us, and it is not for us to find fault with those who do not understand as we do. Does this not make it easier to understand, why mankind is different? Some of us may have hangups, from other lives, which make it difficult this time. Others, have done so well before, they will have very little trouble adjusting to this life.

What an exciting challenge it is, to be able to meet the needs of each soul, as we come in contact with them. This very ability, if it can be mastered, will do much to help you in your rapid advance along the path. Helping others, on this path, definitely helps your progress. This interrelation between all mankind, works to the benefit of the doer, in the name of the Father. Humbling yourself, in the eyes of the Father, will make you strong, in the eyes of your fellow man. What a sense of strength can be achieved, when you remain in tune with the Infinite Power, which has placed you here.

Know the truth, and you will be free. Be at one with the Father, and you shall be free. This isn't much to ask, but it takes so much understanding to grasp the full meaning of these two simple statements. We each, have much to give in our own way. Recognize this, and you will have no trouble in understanding your fellowman. Each in his own way, and the work of the Father is being accomplished, in a beautiful, harmonious way. You are now in a position to be a big help, in making this a better place for all mankind. Each has a small bit to offer to the whole, and this makes up the complete plan. Our purposes all mesh beautifully together, into an integrated whole. No one, is more important than the other, but we are a part of this total picture. Which drop of water, in a lake, is the better? This is a most important aspect, of the teaching of the masters. How important it is, to know of the oneness of all mankind, with the Father. We all have the divine spark, and this is good to know. Without this knowledge, how could mankind ever begin to resolve his differences? We must all realize, there are no differences. In the beginning, was the Father, now, all is of the Father. There is no other. This is all there is. Realize this, and you can never be separated from the Father again, ever. Any separation, comes from you, not from the Father. This is your making, not his. You cannot help but be saved when this is fully realized. What a wonderful feeling this is, when the full meaning of this statement is realized. All is in harmony, when you have reached this level of thinking. The angels, masters, teachers, and guides are all praising the glory of this moment, when it occurs.

Rejoice, and know that I am. You may say, "How can I be so far off base, when I know this is so?" Knowing, and believing, are two different things. We may know, or be aware of many truths, but accepting them completely, is another thing. We must first, have no reservations about the truth. Then we must let it fill our being, to a full, complete saturation of this truth. There must be no room for doubts, or unsureness, concerning this truth. When this point has been reached, then, and only then, can you begin to fully appreciate the truth for what it is. Once this point has been reached, there is no room for negative doubts entering your consciousness. Only the truth will persevere. Only then, can you truly be free. What a beautiful feeling it is to know this has happened so completely, that you have truly been saved. Rejoice, and know that you are of the Father now, tomorrow, and forever. You will surely see the creations of the Father, in a different light. It will be, as if a bell has rung in your consciousness, or a light has finally been turned on within, and made to shine for all to see.

We must all receive this blessing, before we begin to move up the path at a faster pace. This must be accepted without reservation. It must be understood that this must be so for all time. This is not something that you can mouth, but must be something you feel, to the core. How could you fail, with this knowledge? How could you fail to sense the change that has taken place in your normal relationship with your fellowman? All wonderful things are happening, when this truth is understood. You need not concern yourself, with such basic premises, as the ten commandments, as they are all covered with this one premise.

Accept this premise, and you will sin no more. You need not concern yourself, with what others will ever think of you, as this is obvious. Man will easily see the Christ within you, and this will pave the way for a happy, successful life, as you move among your fellowman. All relationships, will be harmonious, as this has taken place within you. Karmic debts can be erased for all time, once this level has been achieved. Since you have reached this level of consciousness, you have had a profound effect upon the universe. All mankind, has been blessed accordingly, when you have grown.

When you have chosen this path, you must continue to show the progress expected of you, or you will suffer as no man will know. This will be a suffering brought about by yourself. No one else could hurt you, as you can harm your own progress. Follow the truth, and you will inherit the earth, so to speak. Know that I am God, there is none other. Know this, and you will be free. Keep your attention focused only on the Father within. Look to none other for answers, which are to be found within each one of us. Continuing to tune yourself into this inner flow, you will instinctively know, what you need to know about your purpose on this earth-plane. You will instinctively know, what the purposes of others might be, and how they will mesh with yours. Know these things, and your Father's work will be done more effectively. Know these things, and you have moved to a higher position on the path. Know this, and you will be helping souls on all levels, whether of this earth, or not.

CHAPTER VIII

GOD IS ALL THERE IS THERE IS NO OTHER POWER

Now is the time for you to behold the living God in your life. Accept, and know this truth. Now, you can begin to understand the importance of this statement. The last chapter has touched on this, but the full truth must be known, to grasp the meaning of this chapter.

You will be facing many situations in your everyday life, which could make it difficult for you to keep your mind on this truth. It is easy to give power to the material, physical problems, we are faced with every day. How often do you say, "What shall I do next?" or, "Where do I go from here?" These, are among the most common misconceptions we are faced with every day of our lives. Take the first, "What shall I do next?" This is easy, if you will learn to live in the now. Don't be so concerned about tomorrow, but have concerns, and goals, which you are working on, but not so much as, now what? Your plan, will unfold beautifully, if you only let it. Don't push things, just relax and let it happen. When each door opens, give thanks, and enter willingly. You know that you are preparing for the next step in your life, if you are staying in tune with this infinite power, flowing through you. Take the ball, and go with it, when each new phase comes into your life.

Have no fear, or hesitancy, about what part you will play in this universal scheme of things. Know this, and you will be prepared for all eventualities. You will lovingly meet, and cope with all challenges, as you are confronted with them. Each day will offer new, and exciting challenges for you to meet. After awhile, you will begin to look forward to these, and find the results of these encounters, gratifying.

You have asked, "Where do I go from here?" I say, that this is not of your concern, but it is your Father's. It should be your concern, only when you have decided to run your own life, and make your own decisions. Then, and only then, will you have problems. Stay with the basic law, and let the Father be the judge of what your plans should be. Do this, and you will have the answers as you need them. Do this, and you will be one who is in tune with this Infinite Power. How do you know what the plans are, for your life? This isn't as easy as you might think, for many to understand, as they have lived a so-called self made life, up to this point. In order for you to understand what is necessary for you to do, before you can fully comprehend this change in your attitude; you must be a loving, willing servant of the Father. Again, with no reservations, you will be able to see the plan unfold before you.

We may be of one seed, but we are uniquely different. This difference, is the reason we will not all receive this information, in the same manner. With some, the intuitive voice within, will keep sending him the instructions, or the outline of his part in the universal scheme of things. Others, may get this in a dream, or a vision. Others, still, will find this in meditation, with an oral, or visual picture, or both, of the plan. There are enlightened psychics, who can help in this manner, but the answer is always more accurate, when it can come from within the desiring soul.

You can readily see that there should be no fear, whatsoever, when these answers are available to each of us. It is also good for us to know, that your work is not complete, when you have left the earth, but your task still remains for you on other levels. All we can do, is the very best we can, while we are on this plane. If we will understand, that our progress can be much faster on this plane, than in subsequent lives on other planes; we will certainly, want to do the best we possibly can, while we are here. Spiritual growth can be at a much faster rate, on other planes, if we are consciously working with, and helping loving souls on those planes. This in turn, will help your growth on this earth plane. If this seems confusing, more will be said about it at another time, in a later chapter.

This treatise, as it is being given, is an attempt to simplify the simple truths that have been taught throughout the history of man. Much has been written, and much has been said, but little has been done to simplify this truth, so the average man on the street, will be able to understand it. It is important for mankind to know how to achieve this union with the Father. It is easier to see this, if he understands that he already is one with the Father. All mankind must do now, is recognize this basic truth. The teachings, of the returning Christ, will also be as simple, as it is brought forth in this book. Know this truth, and you will be saved. It is as simple as that, yet theologians have made such a big deal of this, all along.

Now, you have reached a plateau in this book, where all of this seems too easy to be true. You might ask how this could be. Even the energy holding the complete universe together, is a simple thing. The smallest atomic structure is being held together in the same manner. Every particle of every cell, is doing its chosen thing. Every organ in the physical body, is doing its thing, and is doing it harmoniously, with the cooperation of all other organs of that body. All are interdependent upon each other, and each must accomplish its purpose in this life. Is this so different, from the purpose we have in this life, in relation to the complete divine plan? One confused cell in your body, will affect your whole system. It is simple, if we can see how a confused soul, who is not pulling his full share of the load, will also affect the whole universal scheme of things, as set up by our Father. You say, its a matter of scale, but the atomic structure of metal, has the same relationship as one galaxy in relation to a corresponding galaxy.

All of this, then, should give you an even greater appreciation of all that surrounds us, every moment of every day of our lives. Every material thing, will be something to give thanks for. Its very manifestation into our lives, is a blessing from the Father. What better tribute could be given to all that we enjoy in our lives. We fully realize, that each material object has been a creation of the Father, through the use of mankind as a tool, to express his greatest good for us all to enjoy. It is his to give, and up to us to accept it in a gracious, loving manner, in his name. Thank you Father.

By now, you should begin to understand the simple, basic premise, that is the thread throughout all existence. This, again, is the one reason for our being. Without this, there would be utter chaos on all levels of understanding. Those, who have not reached a very advanced state of being, will never fully realize the power exerted by those of higher levels of consciousness. They could only learn by one misfortune after another. There would be little, or no spiritual growth on this plane, but this would only occur on other levels, other than this physical plane. Without the need for spiritual growth, man would continue to live in his negative world, hating every moment of it.

What could one look foreward to? What hope could there be for a better world for us to leave for future generations to come? Know, understand, and use the power of the Father wisely, and you will truly, inherit the earth. Much has been said of man, and his relationship to his environment, but I give you a total, loving environment, made of the loving energy of the Father. What better way to enjoy the life, that has been given you? What better way, than knowing full well, the meaning of the presence within. All answers will come from within, all problems will disappear, with the power from within. Man will learn to live with no fear, as he will be able to accept the divine protection that is with him. There is only one way to travel through adversity, fear, and doubts, and that is with the knowledge, that God is all there is, there is none other.

Much has been accomplished during the last century, in scientific progress, but it has only been in recent years, that man has been receptive to the spiritual needs, on which his very existence depends. We are fortunate, however, in the fact that many like souls have returned at this time, to prepare the way for the return of the Christ. These very teachings, are to be forerunner of the teachings we will be familiar with, in the next few years. I am only one small outlet, for the Masters, yet this material, will reach untold souls who are in need of the comfort which the truth will bring. No man can be free, until he will know, and understand the truth.

We are not to preach to our fellow man, but we must illustrate the effects of these teachings by our very presence, and example we would have the world to see. Care not, what others may speak, think, or do; be concerned only, with the fact that your very presence, is helping to raise the consciousness of all those with whom you will contact. If each man has the power of the Christ, then how can we enter the coming century with no hope of peace. If love and peace, become the dominate thought in man's minds, then we will have love, and peace, and not until. Be strong, in the knowledge that you are at one with the Father. This will set you free, and the whole universe, will be affected by this commitment. Man, has the right to choose the kind of thoughts he will have. Let us make these thoughts loving, positive thoughts, about our oneness with the Father; rather than destructive, negative thoughts, which will help no one. This simple dedication, will change you first, then the world.

CHAPTER IX

THE COMING CHRIST IS ABOUT TO REVEAL THE TRUTH OF UNIVERSAL LAW

This is now the time for you to recollect the earlier pages about the truth, and how it relates to the teaching of the Christ. The truth, as you have known it, isn't always as reliable as you might think. How can the truth not be reliable? This is so, because in the past, man has been able to distort this, with his own ego. This may be difficult to grasp, and understandably so, but the fact remains, that man must be able to step aside, and let the power of the Father flow through him, without any interruptions. When the human ego is allowed to interfere, the law can be distorted.

The truth is in reference to the law, only as to the authenticity of the source. The law has been with man from the beginning. The truth has only served to emphasize certain aspects of the law, which will make it easier for man to understand. This basic law has never needed to be revised in any way, but it has needed to be revealed to man, over, and over again. Either man has a short memory, or man has been anxious to follow his own ego into the depths. Think, how great could have been the progress, if man could have had his thinking attuned with that of the Father.

Just the knowledge that this is so, is reason enough for man to turn around, and follow the teachings of the Father. The path may be narrow, but the rewards are many, as you travel this path toward total and complete freedom. The truth is easy to see, if you accept the Father as the creator of that which you survey; both the physical, and the non-physical alike. Another way to express this, might be to say, the visible, and non-visible. Some will only believe, if they can pick it up with their five senses. Others will use the God-given inner sense, which will explain the truth, as never before.

Jesus, was in full command of all senses available to man, and he said, "You will do greater things than this." He knew of the great potential of all mankind, but man has either been unwilling to take up the scepter and go with it, or he has been hindered along the way with self doubts, and myriads of negatives, which hindered his progress along the way. You can, and will, do all that the Christ was able to accomplish. You alone, have to make this decision. The decision is yours. Do it today, and you will be free. Wait, and you will be a prisoner of the negative forces building around you. You, can be a loving master, or a hateful slave. Who, in their right mind, would choose the latter? You will find, at the present, a large majority are with the latter group. It is up to each of us, to do our part in raising the level of spiritual consciousness of all mankind, before the coming of the Christ.

By this time, you will have seen how this law is manifesting itself in the world today. You also know that we are not doing this task alone, but have the help of countless souls on other planes, which work in our behalf. You need never feel you are alone in your progress. Besides the Father, you have his army of assistants, working in your behalf. No man, need ever feel alone, but should be eternally filled with the joy of the holy spirit within. What a glorious way to follow along the path. The path may be narrower than you like, but you will not be aware of this.

Why not believe in the truth of the Universal Law, and what it can do for you. If you fully understand this, you have reached a level of spiritual growth, that few can attain during this life. This law makes all of this existence possible. Without it, there would be nothingness. All that we enjoy, is the result of the working of this law. It is impossible for one to completely disregard the law, as we know it. If this were possible, complete chaos would result. Fortunately, most, however, will bend the law slightly, which is enough to make them live a life of misery. Man cannot exist, and be all bad. There is still the Christ in each of us, no matter what the crime might be, when the law was broken. Be that as it may, we must recognize the good in everyone we meet. What a good beginning, having each one of us doing this, with every soul we meet on our path.

Before you know it, others will have a different attitude toward you. People who never spoke before, will now stop and speak to you for the first time. It will be easy for you to make friends, when you understand the working of the law, and how it can help you. Do not be concerned, when a friend does not think as you do, or will fail to agree on an issue. This is natural, as he is working with the law in his own way, and you must realize this. He, too, must realize that you must also have your right to move along the path, where you are.

All relationships between mankind will inprove, as this becomes evident to all concerned. It need not be a big thing, but it is a great responsibility for us to let our fellow-man be himself. No one is going to think, and act, as you will. We are to give thanks that this is so. If this were possible, by some invention of man, then a serious portion of the basic law would have been broken. Many would suffer the injustice done, were this to take place. If we were meant to look, act, and think alike, then it would have been so all along.

Part of the harmony involved in living, and working with the Universal Law, is the power generated in giving thanks for the many blessings we enjoy. Do this, and you will be repaid many times over, for this thanksgiving. It must never be something you feel obligated to do, but it must be a natural, loving response to the many blessings which you enjoy. This thankful feeling, also is contagious. Do this, and you will have helped others give thanks for their blessings. How could you live a life full of negatives, when you are busy giving thanks to the Father? Fill your life full of loving, positive thoughts, and you will have little time for anything else. Do this, and you will realize your oneness with your Father completely. Every molecule in your realm, will be a loving molecule for your greatest good, when you have already given thanks for it, in his name.

You have come a long way, since the beginning of this book. You have been reborn many times, only to come back for more and more understanding. You will create an insatiable desire for the truth. How could you ever think about criticizing your fellow-man, when you know full-well that he has a right to his place on the spiritual path? You will now begin to see why certain individuals need different approaches to learning of spiritual truths. When man can see the truth, as described herein, there will be no need for these varied approaches to spiritual teaching. The simple truth will be known, and understood. Man will still not be a homogeneous group, as you might think. He may know the truth, but still in his own way. Thank you Father, for this.

When the Christ returns, we will all want to know how this affects us, personally. As mentioned before, we are all affected personally, when a butterfly falls to the ground. How much greater must this be, when the Christ returns. The law, as Jesus taught it, will surely be covered, but the simplicity of the Universal Law, will be emphasized. Our close relationship with the one power, the Father, will also be stressed at this time. The continued journey up the spiritual path, is also an important part of the teaching. This path to ultimate freedom, is the most important aspect of this journey. Know these things, and you will be free. May the light of the Father, continue to shine brighter, and brighter, so that it might be a beacon, telling all mankind, that this is a Christian.

CHAPTER X

WE ARE ALL OF ONE SOURCE

It is time for you to see the light, as the Masters have since the beginning of time. The one root for this universe, and indeed, all universes, has been of one maker. This has all been the creation of one power source, and only one power source is involved. We have a tendency to give power to many sources, as we go through life. You will now see that this one source controls all existence. In the past, man has believed in many sources of power. There was a power attributed to the forces of nature, which in turn, had its own power. Today, we give power to many sources, very much like each home having its own power source for electric current, or each city having its own power source, etc.

We will understand how the suns rays, will have enough energy to make plants grow, but find it difficult to see how that relates to the energy generated from a waterfall. There can be no separation of sources for this energy, which makes all of our physical existence possible. This dynamic energy source, permeates all that we have ever been aware of, or all that we will ever be aware of, in all time, as we know it. Without this spark of energy, we would have a void of nothingness, if that is possible. With this energy, we have mankind placed on many planes of existence; some doing the best they can to work within the basic law, which governs all existence. Others, at the same time, feel free to choose a life, whereby they will not live by the law, but on their own terms, be free men to do as they wish. I say to you, that these men are not free, but are the slaves of their own selfishness.

"Where does all this take us?" you might ask. It does make it possible for man to see the divine energy source in all existence. This is the easiest way for one to progress at a rapid rate in his spiritual growth. One, can never again, view all things about him in the same light that he did moments before. Up to this point in your life, you have only had yourself to worry about, now you have all humanity, which has suddenly become part of your own inner existence. You can never be an island, separated from the world, as you are of the world, in this existence. Once you have begun to grasp this concept, how then, could you ever go back to your older, false beliefs? Once this has been understood fully, you will find it easier to forget the old patterns of thought. You will now begin to understand how simple life really is. This existence, for all purposes, is not for our convenience, but it is for the convenience of a divine plan, which can only survive, in an orderly fashion. You are that tool, which has been fashioned to do a specific task. Do this, and you will be rewarded. Shirk your task, and you will create your own hell.

The true free man, in the coming age, will not see one man better than the other. Man, in the new age, will recognize only the Father as his true employer. All of man's earthly bosses, will become artificial paper tigers, with no authority, if they were not placed in that position by the Father. In some cases, man has assumed the role of leadership when he has not been deserving of it. In other cases, man has been a proven leader in other lives, but has not been given the opportunity to fulfill his destiny, in this life. If such a man has a soul, who has worked diligently, in behalf or the Father, he will be rewarded.

Fortunately, many great souls today, are in positions of leadership, and this is good. More and more, these great souls of the past, will assume the leadership of many peoples, in his name. When a man usurps the power to lead, from a deserving one, he brings with him, great forces of negative thinking, which have power for evil, but not of a substancial source, that will help it endure. We must realize that our true leader, is the Father, who has placed us here. We must realize that we each, must have a job to do, in his name. He alone, is our true employer, there is none other. Do your work in his name, and your earthly employer shall surely reap the benefits. You are being blessed for reading this material, and will be blessed when this thought pattern becomes one that you have accepted. With such a loving thought pattern spread out among the ethers, much positive good, will evolve among the working classes, everywhere. Strikes will be a thing of the past, and man will work harmoniously with his fellowman. There can be no petty politics, or jealousy, when each, in his own way, is working for his true employer. Know this, accept this, and not only will you be blessed, but all of your colleagues will be blessed, as well.

You have seen how man can improve his relationship with his fellowman, with this true sense of his source. Now, you must see how man can become more aware of the physical environment surrounding him, every moment of his existence on this physical plane. The plant, animal, and mineral kingdoms, too, will have much more to offer, when their true source is fully understood. Scientists will be able to see many new possibilities, when this energy source is understood. When the chemist understands that his physical makeup, consists of almost all water, with a few mineral traces, then he shouldn't feel too remote, in a physical sense, from the rivers, lakes, and oceans, which could in turn, be separated into two gases.

Make you feel insignificant? It shouldn't, as your everlasting soul, is the important aspect of your being. Your physical body, is the tool, for your soul to achieve the greatest good, during this existence. This is one or the best ways for you to understand what the whole existence, is all about. Man, is just now beginning to grasp the complete picture, as he fits into the total realm. You are one of the very few, who have been able to get this picture, presented in such a simple manner. With this in mind, you can begin to focus upon a new realm of understanding. This understanding, is what we will need, to prepare us for the coming era. A time when the new Christ has returned, and the way has been paved for his smooth entry into the mainstream of contemporary life. This may not be as easy as one might expect, but it is hoped that this will be an orderly change, for the betterment of all mankind.

It is now clear, how this knowledge of the oneness, will make the transition an easy one for the new Christ. This will be an important aspect of his message for all men. You, who will be here at this time, will indeed be among the chosen few, who will help make this all possible. We are living at a time, when mankind has not been able to progress very far, in settling his difficulties on this physical plane. One of the great hangups, is the very fact that we live in a materialistic society. This society, is one which emphasizes what man can do, not what man can do through the power given him from the Father. When it has been acknowledged that we are the instrument through which the Father does his work, we have begun to put it into proper perspective.

Since we have recognized that our Father, is the source of our greatest abundance, we can not help but know that this is the only source of our greatest good. Man, will no longer look outside himself, for this good that should come his way. We attract this good, when we are able to know that it is taking place through us. Know this, and it is so! Know this, and you will no longer be the same person you were moments before. When you have been able to assimilate all of these simple truths, given herein, you can never be the same. There is no other way for you to advance on the spiritual path, as rapidly as this method.

If you begin to judge your fellowman, or find fault with him, then you might just ask yourself, what makes one drop of water better than the next one? If you have been able to grasp the theory of reincarnation, then, you must understand that you have lived many lives, at various times, and have been many races of people, as well as experiencing both sexes during these lives. How foolish, then, would it be, to ever hold any ill-feelings about one of another race, or sex. It should not be too difficult, also, for one to see how man could be born of one sex, yet have a tendency toward the other sex, in this life. It is not right for us to judge our fellowman in this way, or in any other way. Do this, and you have separated yourself from the oneness with the Father, who has placed all of us on earth, at this time. Each, must answer to his maker, in one way, or another. Let this then, be the way it is handled. Take it upon yourself, and you have begun to make a difficult Karma for you to overcome. Yes, we are being judged every moment we exist, on all planes. Isn't this enough judgement for us? Why do we insist upon playing God, in our judgement of others?

Man's laws, should be based on the Universal Law, completely. This has been difficult, since man has found many ingenious ways to break this Law, and many degrees for which the Law was broken. Also, man must let his own ego enter into law-making. Often, emotions enter into making a law, particularly, if the offended one is a lawmaker, or a close friend of one. Many of man's laws have been instituted because of selfish reasons. When this is the case, the lawmaker has seriously breached the Universal Law. When Universal Laws are obeyed, all mankind is blessed. There should be no law which would help only a select few.

We are now about to enter a phase of the life of mankind, which will be a big help in preparing man for the events to come. It is important to understand why this is the one important facet of man's understanding of how and why he was created on the earth, at this time. All molecules in the universe, are preparing for the advent of the Christ. There will be no stone, or blade of grass, which will not be prepared to accept this wonderful gift of the Father, When this can fully be understood, and only then, will man begin to glimpse the full importance of this event to come. This same preparation was given when Jesus of Nazareth entered this plane two-thousand years ago. This is as it should be, and we know and understand, that this is the wish of the Father that this is so. You are among the select few souls, who will receive this knowledge, but when you do, you must not run around trying to convince others of this truth. Others will know, and understand the truth when they are ready, not until. Our job will be to be that good example, which is so necessary at this time, in the history of man.

The vibrations of the universe, will be reaching a fever pitch, when the Christ returns. You, must be ready to help others understand what is taking place, when that time arrives. Many will be confused, and the Christians, who have received the light, will be able to help clarify the true purpose of the return. We must fully realize that the souls who do the menial tasks around you, are truly your brothers. There can be no mistake, man must know for all time that this is so.

Man, also must understand that all of God's handiwork surrounds him at all times, during his existance on this earth plane. You will begin to feel at home with existence, whether or not you have been aware of it before. Every material object, which is useful to you in your daily life, will respond in a different light, when this understanding has been achieved. As we come closer to this full realization, we will be existing on even higher levels of consciousness, than we could have ever dreamed of. Know this oneness, and you will inherit the earth. Your place will be a revered one, in which many souls will be lifted to the heights, because of this understanding. Know these things, and you will be free. Know these things, and you will see God. All existence will relate to you. You will have no fear of God's gifts ever being taken from you, and you will be blessed by the bountiful gifts of the Father. It is his wish that you are made happy, and that you will never want for anything. This will be true, only if you are able to realize how this simple law of acceptance and giving is working in your life, every moment of every day.

Every seed, every leaf, will joyfully become at one with you, if you have allowed it to be one with you, first. This is a natural law of attraction. It is a law which will draw all material things unto you, if it is used wisely. If this is not used wisely, these elements will be repelled by your presence. The animals will lovingly give their lives, so that they too, might also become a part of your existence. We already know the white corpuscles lovingly give their lives, in order to cleanse the body of diseased tissue. These are among the smallest allies we possess. These small allies, can relate in many ways. Every molecule in your automobile, will respond in a loving way, when the starter switch is turned on, or when the accelerator pedal is pressed downward. Many millions of molecules, all shapes and sizes, are responding to your command. How would these same molecules react, if you cursed your car, or thought only of the times your car wouldn't start, or any other negatives you might conjure up. You will get a different response if you would curse your plants, instead of praising them. The same would go for your pets, or your family. Why repulse all existence outside of yourself, when this is only separating you from your source. It has been said many times before, that you will never truly be separated from the source, you will only think you are. God is with you always, even when you choose to live in a pool of negatives. One can never leave the presence of the Father, he will only be hypnotized into believing this is so. Why kid yourself into believing that you could live a life of evil, when you could turn it around and live in the oneness.

CHAPTER XI

YOU HAVE BEEN ON EARTH FOR EONS OF TIME

It is time for all men to realize what their background might be. Most, think of themselves, as souls who have lived only one time. This is that time, but they have failed to realize what their full heritage might be. Some are so wrapped up in their family heritage, that they have little interest, or room in their hearts for knowledge of their full past, consisting of many lives, on many planes, and levels of consciousness.

This is so important, that you know more about your own past, that much is being done to help make this knowledge more easily known. Many books are being written, which will help explain the phenomenon, but this only scratches the surface. Most of us have been here many times, and have come in contact with those we meet every day, sometime before in another life. This is a wonderful way to become acquainted with the past, with the many souls you are meeting every day. Why not become aware of this vast amount of heritage, which is truly yours? You will understand why you have been reincarnated with those around you, which make up your present life. This is all part of the divine plan which is set up on higher levels, and which tends to control, to a degree, the activities of mankind on the earth plane. It is true, man does have the right to make decisions, which will affect his life, but those very decisions, are learning situations, which are needed to help with the progress of a specific man.

Will you now just relax, and let the power of the Father flow through your very body. This is an exhilarating feeling, just knowing that this power, is the same power that flows throughout the universe. How can one be aware of the universe, without this exhilarating feeling. It is the very feeling that instills life into a plant, an animal, or all inorganic matter. We have all been in tune with each other, many, many times before. Some, will love a little wild flower because it is one they have been close to many times before. Some will be familiar with geographical locations, as they have been in those places sometime before. You are apt to meet souls you have been close to, many times before. Often, those meeting for the first time during this lifetime, will both recognize each other instantly. These souls, are not looking at the physical attributes alone, but they are seeing the soul of the ages. This is the one, true way, man can really identify other men, when they meet. Those who have developed a psychic awareness, will always be able to see his fellow man in this light. Someday, man will have this ability, and it will be a common thing for you to recognize your friends from many, many lives before. This, then, is the true heritage, that man should be seeking. We have been fooled into thinking that one's own family history is the most important aspect of his being.

You can now be free of this, and begin to understand more of the true history of mankind, as it has been told in the Akashic records. This is the accumulative record we have made during all existence, which includes all levels of consciousness, and all levels of attainment. You are being judged by those of a higher order, under the direction of the Father himself. This alone, is enough reason for man to stop judging his fellow man. This is another reason, why you must look to the Father for your direction. Do this, and you have become one who can do all things in his name. What freedom! It is easy for you to see why this is possible, when you have experienced so much before. You are the sum total of all that you have been, or ever will become. This is good, and is as it should be.

It is time for you to be able to understand what it means to go back in time, and get a glimpse of your heritage. Much has been written, but little of it relates directly to you. You will always say "How can this affect me?" This is easy, as all things that have ever happened on this earth are always affecting you. You are constantly being bombarded with the energy waves of all past and future experiences that have ever taken place, or that will ever take place in the future. This is easier to understand, if you will know that there is only the now, in the sense of time, on all higher planes. We alone are the ones who divide time up into the past and future.

You can rest assured, that this is not an easy thing for one to grasp for the first time. You will, however, be able to see this in a better light, when you have begun to experience the past and future, while existing in the present. Once you have begun this travel, you will see how easy it is to be able to move in all levels of consciousness. Most of us are trapped in our physical bodies at this point, in time, and it is possible to be freed from this concept of thinking. We have been hypnotized into thinking that this is all there is. What a fallacy. You might say, "This is all well and good, but how can I get to the point where this is all possible to understand?" Nothing comes without some effort, but you can be rewarded if you but begin to think this is possible in the first place. Next, you will do some reading, and find out more about the advantages of regular meditation.

This quiet period in your life, should become the most rewarding time you will spend every day. Pick a time when this is possible, and use a comfortable chair, in a pleasant room. The surroundings are of utmost importance for the beginner. You will now need to relax completely, and this can best be done by inhaling, and exhaling deeply, then relaxing the whole body. Begin with the head, then follow through the shoulders, and the chest. Inhale, and exhale deeply, but gently, then let the arms relax completely, from the upper arm, down to the lower arm, and the hand and fingers. Repeat the same process, and relax the abdomin, back, mid-section, and the legs. When you are completely relaxed, you may take another breath, and feel yourself going into a deep sleep. You will wish to remain conscious during this experience, and this is good. You will be able to see a blank screen upon which all of the events will be shown. You will begin to see a picture develop, and this may be the guides who are aiding in this quest. You will be able to hear audible voices, and often, you will begin to see colorful scenes, which will be telling you something you need to know. Much instruction can be given, as you relax in this position of meditation. It is important, that you will know that you are in the hands of the Father, when this meditative state is reached. Many are not wise enough to realize this, and the energies of lower level souls can enter in to confuse the messages thus received. This is important, to always realize the power of the Father flowing through you, for the greatest good to all concerned. With this in mind, you can grow at a tremendous rate, as you move up the path toward total awareness. You have now begun to rise in consciousness, as you have read the words on this page.

Now is the time for you to be at one with the creative energy of the Father, every moment of every day. No longer, will you reserve the Sabbath, as the day for remembering the Father. You will be finding yourself getting in tune with the infinite power of the Father, whenever you will have a quiet moment. You may be doing a menial task, but no matter how trivial the thought might be, you are always open to the power of the Father flowing through you for the greatest good on the earth plane. How can anything but the greatest good befall one who keeps the commandment, "Love the Father above all." This is all there is, there is none other. This is such a simple commandment, yet, how many can really begin to understand the full impact of this statement. This is one of the greatest undertakings of the soul, as it continues its upward climb on this path.

We are in the midst of a great evolution in the thinking of man.

This is now, only just coming to the fore, as it is being unfolded in the manner which will help the spiritual development of all mankind. This, is one reason the world is so full of negatives, at the present time. These negatives are necessary, as man begins to overcome this method of thinking, and begins to realize the full power of being at one with the Father. More and more, man is realizing his innate ability to meet these challenges, and to be able to put these challenges in the hands of the Father. When a problem is difficult, or seemingly impossible, this technique is always a sure method of solving those problems. We have all been in a position, where all seemed impossible, but it seemed to clear up overnight. This is because we have had the help of angels, Masters, and teachers, under the loving guidance of the Father.

Some are just in tune, and can do no wrong, while others, may have spent many years studying, and practicing the truth, before they will be able to use this great power. Much of this, has been the result of many incarnations before, and some souls may have reached great levels of spiritual development, while, others may have shown lives of regression, and slow spiritual development. With this in mind, you will be be able to understand why souls are existing on many levels of consciousness, and many souls are not ready for the understanding you have understood to be so simple, and easy to understand. It is not up to you to find fault with those who obviously are not on the same level you may have attained. Your very effort to judge them, as they travel the path, will only tend to pull your soul into a lower orbit, than before. Know this, and you will have no difficulty, in seeing only the good, in your fellow man. You will again be free, in another sense.

Have you often felt you may have known, or seen someone before; you may have, as you both have been together before. Have you felt that you have been somewhere before; well, you very well may have been there at an earlier time. Now you have a better idea where you can begin. If you meet many interesting people, during the course of the working day, you very well, may be meeting those people, as part of the divine plan. They are drawn to you, and you to them; as part of the functioning aspect of this great plan. How you react to the situations you encounter, may very well determine whether or not you will continue up the path in a rapid, or slow pace. Using your mind for good or evil, depends upon you. If you keep the commandment, "Love thy Father," you will have no feel of the correct decisions being made. In all cases, you must make your decisions, with the good of all concerned, in mind. Do this, and you will inherit the earth; so to speak.

You will not be able to be at one with the Father, if you have failed to realize the importance of forgiveness, and to understand the workings of the law regarding reincarnation. This law is the one thing, that makes it possible for man to continue up the path, after he has left this earth plane. The learning, and serving, of the Father, continue as before, after the soul has shed the physical body, for a light, airy existence. If man could only feel the freedom he would possess, when he sheds the physical body for the light, ethereal one, which gives him a complete sense of freedom; he would wish to leave this plane instantly. It is understandable, why man usually cannot see this clearly, while he is moving on the physical level. For many, they are very much wrapped up in the physical, because, they are'nt ready for the freedom to be obtained on other levels. Many, will sense this, and even experience the freedom of death, sometime before they are ready to move out of this plane.

Now you can understand why so many will not be afraid of death, and at the same time, why others have a deathly fear of death itself. On the one hand, a man will believe that he has eternal life, and yet, others will only see that this is the only life they will have, and they must get the most out of it. This getting the most out of life, may very well lead a soul into a life with little, or no spiritual advancement. Know that you have eternal life, and you will be free of yet another fear. One by one, all of the negative fears will be leaving your consciousness. What a wonderful way to know how the Father works through us. Know this, and you are one who is destined to do much good, as a loving follower of the Father. Ask, only that you may be a loving servant. This is all you must do, if you wish to be one of the chosen ones who are helping to carry out the work of the Father, on this level.

You are not alone; you have the backing of countless, loving souls, who have been with you many times, and who are working in your behalf. This may be hard for you to understand at first. It will become understandable to you, as you continue your movement up the path. You may realize that you have been in touch with these many souls on many planes, at various levels during your stay on the physical plane. Yes, you have seen many people you may have thought you have known before. This is only because you have been with them many times, in other existences. You will now realize the importance of relating with all levels, as you cannot separate yourself from them, if you should choose to do so. This alone, will give you a feeling of closeness with all levels of consciousness, as you have never before been aware of in the past.

By now, you have begun to realize the importance of being in tune with the infinite, at all times. This does'nt just mean, on Sunday, it means what it says, "always." With this in mind, you will move at a rapid pace, as you travel. This upward movement, will be the most important, single thing, that you can do for your spiritual growth. All else either relates to, or is sub-servient to this one great goal of all mankind. Be at one with the Father, and you will have reached the ultimate in advancing the cause of the Father, as he works through man, for the betterment of all concerned.

It is time for you to remember why you were sent here this time. What was the real purpose in your coming to this plane at this time? Each of us has a job to do, but you will say, "How do I know what is expected of me?" This is only a natural question, and you should know. You will know, if you only will learn to go within, and know the truth, as it is manifested through you.

This too, is one of the ways you can be free, as you move on this upward path.

Now you will not have the remorse, you formerly did, when a friend has left your plane. You will fully realize, that this soul will be waiting for you, if you need this comforting, when you cross-over. You will know that all mankind will be working, moving, progressing, and moving up the path, to the fulfillment that is the rightful goal of all men.

As you reach higher, and higher, you will find these truths easier, and easier to follow. No longer will you be bound by the negatives that have bound you for centuries. No longer will you feel trapped by the problems that beset man. You will truly be one who has reached the Christ image, that is essential for all men to achieve,

Remember, that as you continue to grow in stature, you will be helping pull man up another notch, as all mankind travels up this path. It is not too bad that all men cannot be on the same level of consciousness. If man were on the same level, there would be no great challenge lying before us, as we move along.

We may not like what we see, when we are born into this plane, and it is possible for us to do something about it. God's plan, calls for the gradual improvement of all man, but this rate of travel, is determined solely by the individual involved. What a wonderful way to pace yourself. You can either go like a house-a-fire, or you may choose to regress for a life or two. Be this as it may, you have this choice, and you can determine just how rapidly you will wish to travel. You will also be rewarded for your patience in regard to this matter of growth during many eons of time.

It isn't easy for the average person to fully comprehend, For this reason, many have returned to earth, as teachers. Teachers are returning every day, and they will help carry the message from the higher planes.

It is now time for man to fulfill his destiny on this plane of existence. This can better be done, if man will realize the purpose of his being here this lifetime, and what it means in his total development. This realization can only come with the proper insight into the inner-self. Meditation, is the one sure way of achieving this in an easy manner. Once you have realized the oneness of all time, you will find it is easier to see everything in many perspectives, both looking to the past, and the future in relation to the present now.

You have much to achieve in relation to your relationships with your fellowman. It is important for you to understand your relationship with those with whom you have been in contact, during this life. When this is fully understood, you will see your companions in a new light. One that is easy to understand, one that is, because they too have reasons for being here at this time and place.

You may now presume that you are here for the purpose of making life for mankind, an easier one: one in which man has learned to live with the Universal law. This may sound like a dream that will never come true, but man is being guided in the direction of this perfection, whether he likes it or not. If more and more men will only be aware of this, they will be able to keep in tune with this large amount of aid coming from higher levels.

Being able to utilize this aid, means you have reached a level of consciousness, big enough for you to put this to work in your behalf. How much more good could be accomplished if this were known. This intricate network of aid for each other, on all levels of consciousness, is the reason some souls are able to accomplish so much more on this plane than others. You may think that some put so much energy forth, for such small results. This might very well be the case. Some are to tap this source, and miracles will take place in their lives, daily.

There is much more to the true history of mankind, than first meets the eye. We are complex units made of billions of minute particles, yet they all must work in harmony with each other. The various souls who continue to work together, on this, or on other levels, are still working for the good of this universe, and indeed all universes.

Understanding this simple method using the microcosm in relation to the macrocosm, it is all a matter of scale, that is all. It is easy for man to accept the microcosm, but difficult to grasp the meaning of the macrocosm in relation to the universes, or constellations surrounding us. No one, need ever feel that he is alone in this world. What a joy, to feel this oneness with all of the universe. What a family, you will learn to enjoy. The very tuning in, will open the doors for you to these levels, and you will benefit from the varied backgrounds of these souls, who have completely different backgrounds.

Seemingly, you have known of your past lives, but you are not in a position to understand this. The average souls on this plane, are better off without knowing all about past lives. It is'nt too difficult to see how complicated it might be, if all men knew fully, what their past lives consisted of. Even the knowledgeable ones, are only able to recall a dozen or so lives. This mere knowledge, in itself, is'nt as important as one might think. Yes, certainly, you could learn from the experiences of a handful of lives that relate directly to this one, you are experiencing, at the present.

It is good, to have some of this background, but it is not good to dote on it at all times. You may have been a great leader, at one time, but you may have to learn to be patient, and humble, in this life. This knowledge will help you to know of the potential you have, but you must realize this may not be for you at this time. What is right for you, will be unfolding for you, as you continue to travel the path.

It is'nt a good idea, to live in the past, but it is best to look for the doors opening before you, on this path. It is good, that you are living in the NOW, rather than in the past, or the future. How can one begin to concentrate on the objectives at hand, when he has so much to confuse him, from those past lives. It is enough, that you do the best that you can, in this life, in fulfilling your destiny. Do this, and you have grown in stature, as you as you would have never believed possible. This is part of the exciting challenge that awaits you, as you pass through the portals of life.

Why must we always think of our past ancestry, or our past lives, if reincarnation is our concept of life everlasting? All this isn't necessary, if we can only realize our true source, and know that this is the one thing that should be uppermost in our minds. When we realize our source, we begin to realize that all this really isn't as important as we have thought it might be.

Being able to look within, you will find all answers that you will need to complete your life, in a happy, fulfillment of your dreams. Yes, we have had a great many souls, who have contributed a great deal to the history of man, but this isn't important, when you think of this in terms of the growth of a soul, during these many lives, when he has been contributing to the good of all mankind. This is the time for all men to take a long look at themselves, and see why they have or have'nt followed the goals set before them. You may very well look back, and see from the past experiences in this life, and check yourself on the successes, or failures, you have experienced. Failures, as such, need not be failures, if you have been able to learn from them. Every experience, should be a learning experience. This alone, makes this a positive way to succeed in this life.

Will you now just observe, and view all experiences, as learning experiences. With this in mind, you are now able to view all experience as a loving, happy, positive one, in which you could never fail. You will see only success, in all that you set out to accomplish. If all men could view life, in this manner, there would be nothing but happy souls, who would have little or no problems with psychosis, or other neurosis, which develop from the stress of living at this time.

This is one of the best ways for man to grow from a small child, to a full adult. This comparison, is like that of a soul traveling from the early stages, to that of a soul who has reached the highest levels of attainment, in a spiritual sense. You will now be able to see why you have been born here at this time, and place. The real reason for your being, is much clearer to you now, than it could ever have been before. Your periods of quiet, are the periods when these answers will be coming through to you.

This is the real way for man to progress. It is not in a material sense, but solely in a spiritual one. This is part of the beauty of God's creation. It is the very essence of life itself. You will be able to understand why some, seem to be able to endure untold suffering, and thrive on it, while others will have no need to suffer at any time, but will travel through life with little difficulty at all. This is our proving ground, and we are being proven, in the eyes of the universe. How we succeed, or fail, is all being recorded, and this is good, as we are in charge of our destiny, with the loving approval of the Father. You are being blessed, as you travel.

CHAPTER XII

THE LAW OF KARMA AND THE TEACHING OF JESUS

Much has been said, of the law of Karma, but it is time for man to see how it fits into the teaching of the Christ. You will easily understand why Christ died for our sins, because it has been taught in the Christian church, as the real reason for his being on earth at all. Now, you and I know that we have surely sinned, but that sin was a choice we made for ourselves. This sinning is our acceptance of the dark, negative forces at work all around us. If you can but gain something from reading this book, you will be able to resist the negative forces, by not resisting them. This is the same, as the teaching the Christ taught 2,000 years ago. He, also said, "You are truly in charge of your destiny." If you will accept the negatives that come into your life, as exciting challenges, you will surely overcome them. No, you have not run away, but you have taken the power from the negative, and have given it a positive challenge.

You may have had many lives, in which you lived a life of sin. This very experience, during these times, has made you a stronger soul, who can withstand the challenges of negative forces, as they will bombard you. You will find it easy to live a life of relative ease, in which, you are living in harmony with Universal Law.

Others, who haven't arrived at the level of consciousness, that you have, will be burdened by those very negatives, that have no effect on you. It may seem easy for you, but to others, it is a life of Hell, a life, so full of negatives, they must escape, either by suicide, or mental disorders. It is in everyone's power, to be stronger than the negative forces, and live a loving, positive, life.

Christ, showed us the way, and we have made it difficult to follow; only because we have failed to have complete faith, in his teaching. With this faith, you can do all things, and more, than did the Christ. This is the wonderful heritage, he has left us. Take up this challenge, today, and go forth, in his name, beating down all negatives, that get in your way. Not only will you win, but you will win, with the help of all the hierarchy, working in his behalf. No longer will you feel you are alone in this battle. Not only are you being elevated in your spiritual growth, but you will find that souls, on all planes, will be rewarded, as well, for coming to your aid. Even I, Master Robert, will grow, and move to a higher level, for getting this message through to mankind. All existence, is completely interrelated. We are truly one with each other. This is the only way, there is no other way.

Each of us, has the opportunity to clear up any Karmic debt. This can be done, in an instant, but only if the soul believes, with all his heart, that this change has been made. God forgives instantly, but have you learned to forgive as readily? Have you, also, been able to refrain from judging your fellowman? It must be remembered, that God, is our sole judge, there is none other. You are not being judged, because you wear nice clothes, or associate with the right people; no, you are not judged on a material, physical basis, but soley on the relationship you have with the Father, who has placed you on this plane, at this time.

We, alone, make our Hell on earth. Some seem to need this, but you may grow without it. Those who need it, often will grow spiritually, by leaps and bounds with the challenges offered with such a life. Some will willingly and lovingly, give their lives for their loved ones; so that they might have a spiritual experience, that will change their lives. This sacrifice, usually, is not even in the conscious level of the generous soul, but rather, may relate to a Karmic debt from a lifetime before, or just because of a long time, deep-seated love for the loved one. This loving, sacrificing, soul will be growing at a rapid rate in a spiritual sense. We have all learned to think of these loving souls, as those, who died of an incurable disease, at such an early age. It is always noted, as a great tragedy, but, in reality, it can be a blessing, for all concerned. This is easier to understand, if you can only feel that the loved ones who have left this plane, are not truly out of our lives forever. They are truly closer, in a sense, than they could have been, on this plane.

Many souls, are not nearly as old, as others. These young souls, are those, living on the emotional level of a materialistic society. Older souls, are those who may have been returned several hundred times. This includes lives, where the soul may have shown considerable progress, during a life, or may have regressed one or more lives together. Christ was showing us how to live above the physical plane. The earthly pleasures, were not for him. His sole responsibility, was to the Father, who sent him. Christ knew he must fulfill the prophecy, and this he did. He was not worried about himself, but only was concerned about his relationship with the Father that sent him.

This is the time, when all men should be aware of the truth, as it is given to all mankind. This truth is given to man, in many forms. Some, are only aware of this, when they are in the sleep state; while others are aware of the truth during all their waking lives. The latter is the way for all men to aspire to. It is the one way to complete salvation. This, alone, is the way to be free, to be saved, in his name. This truth is what the Christ was referring to, when he spoke to the Pharisees. It is the truth, he referred to in the parables, which were the riddles of the day. Living, according to Universal Law, means you are tuned into the truth, as it should be. It is hard to understand how man could stray from the truth, when he knows he must answer for it someday. This is the law of Karma, and it is one that can be repealed, only if man is willing to submit himself completely, to the power of the Father, who has sent him to do a specific task.

If man is willing to be a loving servant of the Father, all of his negative forces will be completely forgiven. It is true, that the Father, will forgive, many times over, yet some men find it difficult to forgive one time. No wonder, mankind has such a difficult time, keeping from building negative Karmas. Certainly, man has never been able to completely live in the glory of the Father. Today, more and more, man is beginning to grasp this simple solution to a difficult problem. This is a problem that has plagued man for eons of time. It is a problem that seems to be improving, as the time draws near for the return of the Christ.

We have a great responsibility in keeping the faith, in a time when mankind is concerned with the material world he lives in. many are concerned with the energy crisis, or the supply of food for all mankind. They are preoccupied with these temporal matters, and have lost the true meaning of the faith that should be reserved only for the Father. If you live in the Grace of God, you will have no cause to be concerned with these menial matters. Those who truly believe the teachings of the Christ, will surely inherit the earth. Certainly these will be the chosen ones to lead man into a new era, an era which will make all men free from all negative and evil thought; an era in which man will look only to the Father for his answers. Yes, Jesus showed us the way, and this way is the only way to seek the truth. This truth alone, will set you free. This is a decision that man must make for himself. It isn't a decision to be made one day, and broken the next. This decision must be made for an eternity, once it has been decided.

You can readily see why some men have all the breaks. This isn't just good luck, but it is the accumulation of positive, loving action, completely in harmony with God's law. With this complete and utter childlike faith, all things are possible in his name. It must be remembered, that this luck comes to those who use this law with nothing but good to all concerned. This law cannot be used for selfish purposes, in any way. With this in mind, man will surely learn to live in complete harmony with the laws set down by the Father. Man was never meant to live in poverty, disease, or in want of anything his Father has the privilege to give him. With these rewards in mind, how then, could man still make the decision to follow the path of worshiping many Gods. This includes the Gods of material values, selfishness, greed, power, and an ego that puts him on an equal basis with God himself. This alone, is enough to set a soul back for several lifetimes, unless he has been able to correct this attitude completely. As the Christ stated, "All things are done in his name." When you can fully realize this, you have been able to see yourself in the true light, which is as it should be. For all these many blessings you enjoy, you must never fail to give thanks, in his name. With these teachings in mind, you will surely live in the grace of the Father, forever.

You need not concern yourself with the Karma, or the Akashic records you have accumulated to this time. All of this will surely be taken care of, when you have learned to live God's grace. You may say that people you know are living a life of luxury, while they are living a life of sin. This may be so, but it is the sole problem of that soul, not yours. Don't sit in judgement of your fellow man. Others, may need to make a lot of money, to learn how to manage it for the good to all concerned. This may be their own object for living at this time. Higher souls, who are teachers, or masters, working within the framework of the laws of our Father; may judge you, or others in his name, and under the direction of the Father.

It is time for you to know that you are the sole soul on this plane, at this time, with your goals and obligations to work out in this short space of time. It is a wonderful thing that you are an individual; one which can and does have the option of making mistakes, or living the perfect life. This is as the Father has planned it. You must advance at your own pace, not at a pace set by other men, who have a different set of values to work from. You will know instinctively what your destiny will be. This has been programed into your consciousness, from the time of your entry on this plane. Some will be able to advance far on the path only when they have to suffer, and live a life of difficulty; one which is surrounded with negative forces that abound today. Who is to say one's life style is not good for him? We are solving the problems which confront us, for reasons only the great planner would understand.

It has been necessary to have untouchables, only to give some an opportunity to learn and grow much from this experience. That very soul may have led a selfish life before, one which meant he was in a position to lord it over others who might have been trying to help him. Very often our best laid plans may go astray, only because the negative forces have been allowed to develop.

If you give no power to these forces, you will find they will have little, or no adverse effect upon you. This very living with the positive aspect of life, gives you the confidence which is needed to meet the demands of living in the twentieth century. This is part of the message given by the Christ, when he said that you must never fight the forces of evil, but to embrace them completely. Do this, and you have mastered the one problem which confronts many souls today. You need never have any fear of these evil forces, when you are living the life under the grace of God. With your consciousness so full of the loving, positive methods of living according to the plans set up by the leaders of this plane, and indeed, all planes of existence.

It is time for man to follow the teachings of the Christ, and go out into the world with an open mind full of love for his fellow man. Do this, and you will surely inherit the earth. Much has been written, and much has been said, that you must follow the commandments of the Christ in order to be saved. The commandments to which I am referring, are important, only for those who have no sense of direction. Those who have a definite purpose for being here, at this time, must follow their consciousness. Since we all are individuals, we must be individuals in every respect. The commandments are generalities for man to follow, but it may be, that you have a destiny with a greater purpose, which means that you may have to break one or more of these commandments, in order for you to achieve the goals set before you. These commandments, are only guidelines to lead you generally up the path. Your own set of commandments, set before you for this life, may be quite different from those generally set down for mankind. All you must do, is look within for these goals, and directions. Much can be learned from your dreams and meditations. There are many spiritual mediums who are able to see these goals that have been set for you to achieve.

Once you do understand what you must achieve while you are on this earth, you must realize that certainly the doors will be opened to you for the purpose of achieving these goals, but you must institute a plan of action to achieve these goals. It will do you no good, just sitting in meditation day after day, with nothing creatively being done. Living the life of a disciple, means you must be a spiritual doer, as well as a spiritual soul, in harmony with the divine plan. We should all be the loving servants of the Father. With this in mind, you will not need to concern yourself with the commandments, as they will automatically be obeyed when you are living in Grace. Placing yourself in the hands of the Father, means that you are no longer a separate entity from the Father, but you have truly come home, as the prodigal son.

Living to be at one with the Father, only means that you have increased the tempo of your growth, as you proceed up the path. When you fully realize that all souls are at different positions on this path, you will see how difficult it would seem to be for one man to judge another. This judgement can only come from a higher level than we are accustomed to. Leave the judging of your fellow man to those who are qualified, on a higher level of existence. This will leave your mind free, and clear to do the things that are expected of you without a lot of clutter. Know that you are truly at one with the universal spirit, and you will automatically open the doors which will manifest this very thing. Each of us can and should accomplish greater things, in his name. This is the only way this can be achieved. Drop your own ego, and give the credit to the Father. Once this great channel has been opened, you will feel a sudden surge of energy, which will fill your very being with the joy and happiness of living in Grace.

You will work and accomplish things which you never dreamed possible. This energy of the Father will eliminate the need for sedatives, and uppers and downers, in controlling your emotions and energy level. Rely on the energy of the Father, rather than the energies derived from the drugs which are used extensively today.

It is good that you have begun to understand what it means, to be in tune with the Infinite Power within. This is a glorious way for man to realize his full potential as a soul on this plane. You will never fully realize the importance of this, as it relates to man and his progress, as he moves up the path to total freedom. You, and I, have much to learn, but it is being made much easier for us by information, and materials coming from other levels of existence. This is as it should be, as we are all inter-related. We are entirely dependent upon each other for our very existence.

It takes all levels of consciousness, and all types of souls, to make our society function in a feasible manner. Understand this, and you will know of the secrets which surround all mankind. It has always been here, but few are able to visualize this. The more of the truths that you can understand, the more rapid will be your advancement. Great souls have never moved rapidly along the path alone, but are always in tune with an infinite number of souls, on all levels of existence. Know these things, and you will be at one with all existence. Learn one universal secret, and you will never again be the same person you were moments before.

It no longer need be a difficult task, just being in tune with the Infinite Father within. The concepts in the pages of this book, are designed to make this all possible for the laymen on the street. It should do much toward changing the consciousness of all men. You might say, "How does this all effect me?" It may either make you a happy, healthy living soul, who is full of joy, or you can remain in the groove which has taken many years to wear in, and in which you might say you feel comfortable, just remaining in this groove, without making any effort to get out. Make the simple decision to break from your old behavior patterns, and you are free. You have the option to either plant the seeds of an abundant life, or a life of misery. You say, "Who would be crazy enough to choose the later?" Look around you, and you will see how many have chosen the later. Some will choose the later only because they have a Karmic debt to work out, and this will help make that correction. If this be the case, then you must realize that you can be free instantly, by merely realizing the truth. This is merely an adaptation of the simple truth, as it was given to us by the Christ. It is as important today, as it was two thousand years ago.

We are now undergoing a great change in the consciousness of of all mankind. This change is being made manifest by the many loving, eager souls on all levels and all planes. This interrelationship creates a powerful force for good. This is a force which no man can repel. The physical, material level of consciousness, must always give way to the truth in spiritual levels of consciousness. As this occurs, you will see that the level of man's consciousness will have been raised considerably. Each man, who is transformed, will in turn, transform many others by his example. No one ever need extol the teachings of the Christ to all men, but the work will travel like wildfire, when a group of spiritual souls will only live the truth, as they know it.

It is now time for man to make the decision for good, on this plane of existence. This will eliminate the negative tendencies of man to solve all problems of a material manner, with their own egoes. This separation, alone, is what is causing the difficulties in the world today. We must all learn to be open, free, channels for good on this earth plane. We must truly be as little children, having total faith in the workings of the Universal Laws. This will eliminate all doubts, fears, worries, or concerns about obstacles which befall us as we travel. The challenges, and obstacles, are set up for us to solve, and they will be solved in an effortless manner, only if we will let go and let the Father take over completely. This later solution, is the one solution man has striven for, for eons of time. Unfortunately, man, as he has evolved in a physical, material, and scientific sense, has taken the credit for these advances soley, and completely, through his own ego. No matter how man has tried to separate himself from the creator, he will find only he has left God. God will always be with man throughout all existence. The mere fact that man has this right to decide what his destiny might be, shows how much freedom our Father has given us. When we choose the self, we are loosing our freedom, and when we are loving servants of the Father, we can be completely free.

All that we experience in our earth experience is the product of the Father. We too, are the product of the Father, as is each drop of water in the ocean. How else then, can man help but be at one with all creation. Do this, and you will enjoy every breath of air, every pebble underfoot, and every beautiful plant, as well as the species of the animal kingdom. How then could one ever be unhappy, when he is in tune with all of God's creation.

CHAPTER XIII

WHY DO WE CARE WHAT OUR PURPOSE MIGHT BE?

You are the one who is in charge of your life. You, alone, are the one who makes the decisions which effect your life, every day you are on this plane. It might be said, that you are the one who is responsible for the good and evil which befall you, as you pass this way. Yes, you can either make your own heaven or hell, on this earth. Live within the Universal Laws, and you will live every moment in complete harmony with all creation. Choose the life o of negativity, and you are living a life of sin. This is a simple way of explaining the rule of existing in the grace of the laws of the Father. This is not as difficult to follow, as one might expect. If you will realize that you are the one who is completely in charge of your destiny, then you will be able to let the Father guide you on the path, as it should be. If you should choose, you might feel that you alone, are responsible, in all situations. This is'nt so; in a sense, you are in charge, but must realize from where the power is derived. You are the willing tool, the Father, is the loving entity which is guiding you in all you are to accomplish.

Choose the right path, and you will advance rapidly on the path to complete spiritual unfoldment. Choose a life of negativity, and you will either regress, or show no advancement whatever. We are here, only to prove ourselves to our inner selves, which have worked for eons of time to get this far. Either you can accept the Karmaic background you have inherited, or you may overcome this in an instant. Christ showed us the way, when he said, "Go, and sin no more". It is just that simple. It takes a great deal of determination, for one to remain steadfast, in a decision such as this. If you can honestly say that you have decided to dedicate your life to the Christ, you will have nothing to worry about, as far as remaining on the path, is concerned. This simple statement, can change your life forever. A decision such as this, can have reverberations all over the universe. It is not just something that remains just with you. It is a decision which will make the hosts on all levels, rejoice.

You may wonder what will keep you on the path? It is important to understand that you are not alone, in this struggle for good. Your guides, and guardian angels, and all other hosts on all levels, are all working in your behalf. This is why many are able to remain so steadfast, in this matter. With all this loving help, how can you think of going back to your old ways? We have been led to believe that our God sits on a high perch, and looks down upon us in judgment. Certainly, your Akashic records will show this to be true, to a certain extent, but this is all being done in his name, by those who have such responsibilities. These souls too, are working in our behalf. They too, are urging us to make the correct decisions, which will affect our lives. This alone, will help you to see how important it is to develop a universal consciousness; a consciousness, in which you will be at one with all existence.

The decisions you make on this level, not only effect all levels of consciousness, but they affect the lives of those who are close to you, on this plane. You need not tell all those about you, that you have made such a decision to serve the Christ, they will know this the moment this decision has been made. Those who are ready to live by the truth, will wish to know all about it from you. Those who are not ready, will not show any interest in this, whatsoever. Do not waste your time, trying to convert these people, as they may have to experience these negatives, in order to learn enough to be ready to advance. Some are able to advance at quite a rapid pace, when they live a life of negative thinking, only because they have been able to learn from these experiences. Since we are at various positions along the path, we must be understanding of the soul, who is not at our position.

In order to be in tune withe Universal Law, we must be aware of the fact that we must do all in our power, to bring about the greatest good for all mankind. This means, we must work to help keep a balance between all levels of God's creation, before this can be achieved. We must be aware of energy fields which surround us, and give strength to all existence. The balance between all kingdoms is important. We may be souls who have a direct, conscious contact with the Father. All life must be in tune with Universal Law, or it would cease to exist. The moment we begin to live on the fringes, or outside of this Universal Law, we begin to have physical problems. We may also begin to have mental problems, and will need to consume large quantities of pills, order to calm our nerves. All we really need, is to realize our oneness with the creator. Once this state can be achieved, you will be able to live in peace. We are not to be concerned with how miracles will occur, when we are living within the law. There are no miracles, just the working of the Universal Law, in action. You will not be aware of this, unless you have reached this level of perfection.

You will know when you are about to enter a new phase of existence. You will suddenly be aware of the many forces which affect man in his existence on this plane. These forces are what keep all life, as you know it, in a constant state of change. These changes are taking place even in the most solid of forms. The material world is always changing, and this is good. Life would be rather uninteresting, if existence did not undergo a change. This change is for the good of all man, only if he understands the why of it. We are constantly being bombarded with the forces which enduce change. Our reaction to these forces, is what tempers our very existence, and progress on this plane.

We need to understand the reason for our being here at this time and place. We are here to react and inter-react with those who have been close to us many times before. You have been chosen to be with these souls this time, in order to work out these relationships with them. Thus, it seems, that we all have a reason for our being here at this time. This close relationship, is what makes for the many associations we will have during our lifetime. How we solve the problems placed before us, depends entirely upon us individually. Some of these relationships will undoubtedly teach us something; others will, or should teach us, but we may not be ready for the lesson to be learned at the time.

It is much easier to understand your fellow man, if you understand he also has his problems to work out, and he has his own goals to achieve on this plane, at this time. It is also easier to understand our fellowman, if we know that we are at all levels, as we travel on the path to complete freedom.

How then, are we to know what our purpose might be, while on this plane? One good way to follow the purpose, is to look back over the years, and you will see a definite pattern emerge throughout all life's experiences. Certainly, you may have had many disappointments, and failures, but did you ever learn from these experiences? They were there for a reason. It was something you felt you needed in your subconscious mind. The soul has a long record of experiences, but there are things to be learned, as long as you keep returning to this plane. Some are here to contribute a loving, spiritual lift to those with whom he is to relate. We may have specific reasons for being. Some will live a life of poverty, to understand the problems of those in such a predicament. Others will be in positions of leadership, not only because they are ready for this, but they too, will be able to help many more people, in such a position as this. If man will but open his consciousness to the oneness of the loving Father, he will be in a greater position to do the greatest good possible. Do this, and you will have the help of hosts of souls who are working in his behalf, to carry out the Universal Plan, as it should be done.

You will find that deep meditation, will help give you the purpose for your being here at this time.

This understanding will help you to achieve the goals set before you. You will be able to check, and find how satisfactory your progress might be, to date. Spiritual growth, and understanding, are the most important goals to be achieved, but these can only be achieved by living according to the Universal Laws, set forth by our Father. Living the law means that we must remain tuned in to energy force of the Father within. We must have loving relationships with all entities of this plane. We must care for the entities which are on a lower level of consciousness than we are. Once you have reached this level of consciousness, you will have no trouble feeling the presence of the Father all around you, in all that you will do.

Know that you have grown spiritually, as fast as you possibly can. This is the one important goal you have for yourself. Do this, and you will find all good things will befall you. You will have all the things others keep praying for; abundance, love, health, success, etc. It will not be necessary to keep wishing for all these things to be in your life, if you are in complete harmony with your Father. These things will follow you all the days of your life, without your ever being concerned about them. It is easy to understand why you should live a life with the Grace of the Father, and it is difficult to understand why anyone would ever pick a life of negatives, a life of sin, fear, lack, poverty, sickness, and unhappiness. You will never be the same person for reading this book. You will never be satisfied with the life of negatives you may have lived with for many years. You will now begin to live a full, productive life, as you may never have dreamed of before.

CHAPTER XIV

HOW DO YOU KNOW WHAT YOUR PURPOSE MIGHT BE?

It is time for you to begin to look back upon your life, and see the pattern which has been unfolding. This is the logical place to begin, when you are attempting to find what your purpose might be on this plane. Unconsciously, without your knowledge, you have been following a plan. Certainly, you might deviate from this set plan, but the general trend, and purpose are clearly discernible. It is as if you have signed a contract before entering this plane, explaining exactly what you have been sent here to accomplish. You are probably going to ask, "What are the clues for me to look for, when trying to find my purpose here?" First, you must look for a type of service you have performed up to this time. Maybe you have been sent to learn humility, and this trend of humble service to your fellowman is clearly discernible. You may have been a ravishing beauty before, and took advantage of this fact, so you have been blessed with a plain, homely countenance. You may have been a large, man before, who took advantage of his size, and now you are relatively small in stature. Your physical attributes, are a clear way of telling what you may have been before, and give you a reason for returning to work something out, as you move up your Karmic path.

You may have been placed here at this time, in order to serve your fellowman in making scientific discoveries, or it might be that you can please others by writing a play, poetry, paint a picture, be an actor, comedian, or a talented musician, or dancer. Whatever the purpose for serving might be, that purpose is there. No matter what your method of serving might be, it is important to your fellowman, and it is important that you are serving in such a way, that will speed you on the path.

Each of us has a different purpose for being here at this time and place. This will help explain why it is so important for us not to judge our fellowman. Only God truly knows the real purpose for his being here at this time. His actions often will be paying a Karmic debt one soul owes to another. For this reason, it is important that we not hurt others, as we pass through this life. Many headlines are often the results of deeds done to another eons ago. This does not excuse the soul for performing this act, as nothing has been gained by this, except a Karmic debt has been paid, Solving previous problems in this manner, places the offenders in a negative situation which again must be worked out. If you truly work, and live, in harmony, you will solve all negative problems in a loving manner, with good to all concerned.

It is good to know that all that has happened to you during this life, has been the result of many lives previously lived on this plane. You are the sum total of all of these existences, and you should have shown considerable progress up the path, during these many existences. Just placing yourself in your Father's hands, will mean that you have taken a giant step up this path to the ultimate glory which is thine. It is good, that you have reached a level high enough to want to absorb the material in this book. One's consciousness will rise considerably when it is realized that you must be a part of total existence on all levels.

What a joy it is when you can begin to feel at ease with the many levels in your Father's house. Most, are only concerned with this material existence in this time and space. Tuning in to all levels, will open many channels to you, which you may never have ever considered possible.

The forces of energy which surround you, are constantly being affected by every thought going through your conscious mind. This, in turn, is being transmitted through the ether, for all time. How important it is to live the truth, every moment of your life. Some will say that this is impossible, but it is possible when you place yourself in his hands, completely and without reservation. Be not one who must feel he must prove to the world that he is one who has reached a higher level of consciousness, than those about him. You must be one who lives the truth, but is not concerned with your travel up the path. This will take care of itself, all you must do, is let it happen. Being a loving servant of the Father, is all you need be concerned with. Do this, and you will truly inherit the earth.

Once you have been elevated in consciousness, to the degree that will free you from the negative, earthly cares, you will find this Universal power flowing through you for the greatest good of all mankind. Once you have reached this high level, you will realize that you are only one of many, who are the souls directly in touch with the infinite. Truly, you will be one of many, who are carrying out the divine plans which have been set for eons of time. You will never need to feel you are doing this alone, but you will know that you are being guided by consciousnesses on all levels of existence, who are working in your behalf, according to the Universal plan. Do these things, and nothing but the greatest good will come your way. You will now begin to understand why some of the greatest leaders of the world have been so great. It is basically, because they dare to be different. They dared follow, and work, according to the Universal plan. We are truly indebted to those who have decided to be loving servants of the Father, doing his bidding, without question. Who are we to question the course of action, set before us, for this lifetime?

It is important, that we not concern ourselves with trying to be like someone else, as that someone else you are trying so desperately to imitate, may have a totally different reason for being here at this time. You are a part of a great puzzle, and you are but a small piece fitting into that over all plan. No two pieces of this puzzle are exactly alike, but put them all together, and you have the Divine Plan in action. If one, or a group of us should fail to accomplish our destiny on this plane, the harmonious completion of this plan is seriously affected. Many will not progress as rapidly as one might expect, but again, we are given the sole right of our destiny. We make decisions, some of which will be wise, but others will be foolish ones. It is up to us to learn from our mistakes, and make more and more intelligent decisions, which will help us move rapidly up the path. It must be remembered, that we are not just doing this for self, but we are doing all for the greatest glory of God.

By now, it must begin to seem a little ridiculous that we should concern ourselves with the question of ethnic background. It should be obvious to you, that there is only one Father, and that Father, is God. Not only are we all at one with the Father that has placed us here, but we are at one with all levels of existence on this, and all other levels of existence. This may be of such a large scope, that some will not be able to comprehend this, totally. In time, we shall all understand this basic precept. We shall all attain the highest level of attainment, in due time. You may ask, "Why can't I reach a higher level of consciousness at this time?" The answer is simple, the truth is revealed to you, only when you are ready to accept it. Place yourself in his hands, as a little child, and you will have no need of concerning yourself with the question of being ready for the truth. Christ is one who knew, and fully understood these basic precepts. He was able to tell us in a straight, and simple way, how we could put these truths into action in our lives. You are exhibiting a high level of consciousness, just by reading this material. Those who are not ready, will have no interest in this book.

It is good that you do not concern yourself with those who may not have achieved the understanding you have of these truths. It is their concern, only their concern. Yes, they will be influenced by your advancement, but their growth is their problem, not yours. This does not mean that you should not concern yourself with their progress. You will be able to help others in many ways, as you work with them. You will be able to help those who are falling back, as they move along, and you will be an instrument for good, as you counsel with them. Remember, that you will reach those who are ready for your counseling, but do not concern yourself with those who are not ready for this. This is their problem, and they alone must continue to work this out.

You must continue being a constant example of a soul who has reached a high level of understanding. You will be able to show the way to those who are ready for it, but do not try to convert all who come into your circle, into believing as you do. Remember, their piece to the puzzle will not fit as does yours. You will be able to open the doors, and show the way, but do not try to force, or push others in the direction you think they should take. They all, have various reasons for being here at this time, and they will be plodding along as well as they are prepared to do.

Thank the Father, because all men are here for different reasons, and we all have varied backgrounds built up during the ages. This certainly could be a monotonous place if we were all at the same place on the path, or we had all reached complete universal freedom, with nothing to improve upon. We must always concern ourselves with serving for the greatest good to all mankind, and knowing that the will of the Father, is being done through us. With this in mind, you are ready to be a loving servant of the Father, working in his behalf, with no thought of what is this going to do for me?

Your reward will be forthcoming as you continue to do the work of the Father. It is important not to be concerned about impressing your fellowman about the relative merits you may have earned as a loving servant of the Lord. There are myriads of angelic hosts, and entities on all levels of attainment who are praising your progress along the path. Neither can you fool others, or fail to impress others, if you only are concerned with serving the Father. Nothing else matters, as each of us is progressing up the path to complete freedom.

We are all working and progressing as rapidly as we are able to accept the challenges of attaining a higher level of consciousness. As we continue this progress, we are lovingly supported by the many hosts who are working in our behalf. Our guides and teachers are too, being elevated, as their influence begins to be shown on our development. What a loving thought it must be, to have all souls, on all levels, working in our behalf. This is what is meant by working diligently as a servant of the Father. Our progress is possible, only if many souls are benefiting from the work that is being done, in his name. No longer, will we feel that we must shout to all others, the progress we have made on the path, or how we may have helped others who have had difficulty moving up the path. True, many will meet many obstacles, as they move along the path, and this is for a good reason.

These are all part of many learning situations we must face, as we continue along the way. We all will meet with different situations, and this is good. We are all living our own existence, and this must be uppermost in our minds as we travel. All the more reason for our not comparing ourselves with others we meet as we travel. We each have our own destiny to attain, as we travel. We must all be responsible for our progress, as we alone should know what we have contracted to accomplish in this existence, at this time.

We are all responsible for our rate of progress as we continue. We alone, have the right to make wise decisions, or poor ones, which either speeds or regresses our pace on the path. If we will but open our hearts to all entities who are working in our behalf, we will begin to make the proper decisions which will speed us along the way. The mere knowledge that we are encouraged every step of the way, and rejoicing takes place, as we continue to make headway, means that we are tuning in to the rhythms of the ethers on all levels. How great it is, just to be able to know that we are but a small, but important integral part of the wondrous whole, that we may call the Universal Plan. Once we have begun to understand this Universal force that is working through us for the greatest good of the Universe; we will be able to use this force, this energy, for the greatest good of all mankind. Woe be to the soul who misuses this power. Ask yourself first, is this for the greatest good of all man? If this is so, then you can rest assured that you are working within the law. All decisions must be made in his name, with only the loving service to the Father being uppermost in your thoughts.

We should not be concerned with the progress of those about us, as they are the sole judge of their needs and purposes here, at this time. They are being helped with their contacts with us, and your attainment will be felt by those who are your loving companions in this existence. As your influence for good, is being felt by those about you, their influences on others they meet will extend this power for good to all corners of the Universe. All who you will meet in this existence, will all be part of the Universal Plan, created by our Father. There is nothing which can be considered accidental in our meeting with others who will help us, or will in turn be helped by us, as we meet. This is all part of our total existence, as we continue to work out relationships with loving souls we have known for eons of time.

We must meet every obstacle, as an exciting challenge. One in which we must work out the problems as they arise, never letting them carry over into another existence. All problems must be resolved completely, as they have been placed before us for that very reason. Do these things, and the heavens will sing of praises for you, as a loving son of the Father. Fail to meet these challenges, and all voices will be silenced, as you must continue to face one situation after another, until this can be resolved. More and more, the heavens will be opening up for those who have lovingly accepted those challenges placed before them by the Father. Do these things, and you will truly inherit the earth.

CHAPTER XV

MAKING THE MOST OF THIS LIFE IN GOD'S PLAN

Now is the time for you to make a decision about what you plan to make of your life. You will want to use the power of the universal energy to help make a decision such as this. Tune yourself in to the infinite power within, and you will be the master of your destiny. This decision, and all subsequent decisions, will be made with this universal power within. This is good, as you are always helped in making your decisions, by the many guides who are working with you. Realize this, and you will understand how this power within you works for the greatest good of all mankind. Know this, and you will inherit the earth. If you are one who can instinctively know what his next move will be, you will be working with the grace of God. Those who know and understand the workings of the law, will be rewarded by moving up the path, at a rapid rate. You will advance as few are able to do, only because you have let this power, and this energy work through you for the greatest good of all mankind.

You and I know that the Universal Plan which has been set for eons of time, is important for the advancement of the human race. We have been given this responsibility, only because we are able to tune in with this infinite power, as we do. It is our responsibility to consider all that has been created in this universe, for our enjoyment. We must be at one on all levels of consciousness, as well as all levels of attunement. You no longer will be a lost soul who is groping for the truth, but the truth will flow through you as easily as water flows down a mountainside. Set your ego aside, and you will let the flood of the universal creative energy flow through you.

Those who have achieved this level of attunement, will have reached the higher levels of consciousness. These souls will associate with the greatest souls who have ever trod the face of this earth. You will be at ease with all levels of consciousness. You will no longer be the lost soul you were moments before. You will want to reach higher, and higher, into the upper spheres of the universal realm. You will no longer be satisfied, just being the 8 to 5 P.M. worker, who must keep his eyes fastened to the clock on the wall. You will be living the truth every moment for all time. Once this has happened to you, you no longer will be able to go back to the separate soul, you were before. You may consider yourself born again and again, but you will reach the point of no return, when it would be impossible for you to go back.

You will be able to visualize this infinite plan, and what it means to you, only if you will meditate on this. Go to sleep, with the knowledge that this plan will be clearly shown to you, either in a dream, or a mental picture, the following day. Some will be ready for this information by writing automatically, such as this material is being received, but whatever the method, you are ready to receive information such as this, and you will be prepared to know the plan, and work accordingly. We are only tools, and God is the conductor and director. We are the loving servants, who are following the direction of the Father. We are rewarded handsomely, and the only penalty which we would receive, would be the penalty we would place upon ourselves for not following this direction. Your Father, works in a loving, positive manner. You alone, are the reason for your misfortunes and failures. Your Father, wishes only the greatest good for his children.

You have already been indoctrinated in the basic truth, as seen by the Masters, but you have much to learn about being at one with those on higher planes, who are always at your beck and call, and are the loving souls who are assigned to help you in your travels on this plane. Often, you may think that true miracles have taken place in your life, when you have been served by those who are assigned to work for your greatest good. When this is fully understood, you will be able to work within the law with a richer understanding of the how and why of it all. You will be able to understand why you have chosen the path you have. This is the innate plan which you agreed to work out when you returned to earth this time. Understand this, and you will understand why certain souls have crossed your path during this life, and why you have had such great success along certain lines, but fail when you try to go it alone. Stay within the Universal Plan, and you will always succeed. Let your ego rule your decisions, and you fail, but let God show you the way, and you will succeed. This may sound a bit too simple, but it isn't complicated, only difficult to follow.

We, alone, have the sole right to make decisions, but we also have the ability to work within the law to succeed. You may ask, "Why does anyone choose to follow his own ego?" Man will only do this when he begins to feel he is not of the Father, but that he truly is the Father. The guides who are here to help us in our working out of the plan, find it difficult to help us when we are acting the role of God. If some guides cannot work successfully with us at this, they may be replaced with other guides who will be more forceful, and give stronger direction to your purpose on this plane. As you begin to advance in your spiritual growth, you will find you will need to take on other guides, who will be better suited to help you as you travel on the higher planes. Not only are you with the Father, every day of your life, but every moment of all existence, on all levels. This also means that teachers, and guides are working with you at all times. With this in mind, you could never fail, but you can only succeed. Truly, if you set out to fail, you will surely succeed.

Now is the time to make that great decision which could change your life. You must decide if you are going to continue on a separate path, always feeling that you are in charge, and making all decisions; or you can let God be in complete command, and you be a loving, willing servant, who is willing to do his bidding. The time will come when you will begin to question why you must follow this particular course set up for you. The answer will always be, "Who are we to question how, or why this should be accomplished?" You will begin to accept all challenges placed before you, no matter how menial. When you are able to work in a loving, harmonious way, you will find that those who work with you will see you in a different light. After making a decision such as this, you will never again be the same soul you were moments before. This is the true way to be born again, and you may be born again every day, as you re-affirm your vows to continue being a loving follower of the Father.

Your influence upon those with whom you come in contact, will influence others to make the same decision that you have made, and this influence will continue to grow, and spread, from the first seed, until the field has been completely sown with this seed of love and service. This very thing is being repeated many times over, all over the earth, at this time. This will continue to increase in tempo, until the world will be ready for the advent of the new Christ. This is an exciting time for many of us who will be involved with these events, as they begin to unfold. If we are following the directions of the Universal Law, we will find we are able to help mankind in general; but if we persist in following our own self-directed ego, then we are creating disorder out of order. We are creating confusion, mistrust, and fears among our fellow-man. It is better to help elevate one soul, than it would be to tear down other souls with our ego. How can we hope to benefit, when we tear down, or attempt to tear down others, in order to build our own ego? You cannot begin to build your ego upon a foundation such as this. Your ego will prosper, only when you fully realize that your power comes only from the Father. Realize this, and you will surely be among the leaders of the world. This is a true measure of a great soul.

A big man, need not be large in stature, but only great in his understanding of the power of the Father, working through him. He is only realizing that he is a tool for good. Keep this in mind, and the impossible can be accomplished. Never be concerned with the how about these events taking place in your lives, but only know that it is being done in his name. Those doors will continue to open before your very eyes, as if by magic. Those who have learned to live within the law, will take this for granted, but others will truly consider these events as miracles taking place in your lives.

It is important that one begin to let this knowledge take over completely, and you will have no trouble in meeting the demands put upon you during the course of your life on this plane. You can, and will, be able to live in perfect harmony with all facets of life on this plane, if you will put this knowledge into action, for good to all mankind. Merely being in tune with the

Universal Laws, will help all life on this plane, as you know it. Just being in harmony with your fellowman, is only one facet of the total existence. Our responsibility is to be in tune with all that has been created by the Father, not only on this earth plane, but in a universal sense as well. We must remember that we are important, only as the one seed that has the potential to change the world. Multiply our one seed by many who are on the same level of consciousness as we, and you will begin to understand the great power for good that we possess.

As Christ has said, it is important to be aware of every thought, and every word uttered from our lips. We must realize the tremendous energy generated by these thoughts, and sound waves, as they travel in space. You alone, are in full command of these faculties, and this is the beginning of your transformation into a high level spiritual soul. You are not to follow this instruction only for the satisfaction your ego might enjoy from this elevation to a higher level of consciousness. Nothing will ever be achieved if this is so. You must do this, not for any gain you might derive from this transformation, but only from your being in tune with God's plan for the completion of God's plan for the development of the union of God and man. This goal is the ultimate one for each of us, as we travel along the path. We are constantly making an impression upon our fellowman, as we meet him in our travels. This impression can either be a positive one or a negative one. If we keep our sights only upon serving the Father, we will make a positive impression upon those we meet. If we continue to separate ourselves from the Father, we will, with our ego in control, make a strong negative impression upon those whom we may contact along the path. We do not have to try to impress anyone with our advancement along the path, this will take care of itself. You must come forth only as a natural evolvement on your part. Any phony, artificial affectation will be spotted right away. You will fool no one, as we are all truly in tune with each other, unless we make this definite break with our fellowman.

It is time for you to make the right decision for your life. You have been placed here at this time, in order to complete certain objectives which have been set up for you to accomplish. You are not to question the work that is to be done, but it is up to you to accomplish it, in the best way you know how. This is all anyone can do, but you are doing it all in his name, and need no recognition for the good that is being accomplished through you. Do this, and you will surely be surrounded with the brilliant light of the Father, as you travel up the path. All the angels of heaven will rejoice as you pass through. You will be as the many Saints who have passed this way before you. You will advance at an even faster pace, as the teachers and guides will be working closely with you, as you continue to travel. Never again, will you ever feel alone, but you will sense this assistence which is being offered you, as you continue in this loving service to the Father. You may have wondered why some seem to have all the luck, well you will begin to understand this, as you gain an inner-insight into the workings of the law. This good fortune is always passed to those who remain in tune with the infinite power, and obey the laws of the Universe. Keep yourself in tune with this infinite energy source, and you will have good fortune follow you the rest of your days on this plane. Forget your ego, as it is powerless without the energy of the Father flowing through you for the greatest good of all men. Egos may come and go, but the higher self within, has lived for eons of time, and has a vast experience to draw from. You will no longer feel insignificant, but will know that this higher self is of the Father.

Now you may wish to sit back, and relax, since you have managed to live according to the law. Those who have begun this upward climb, will find that it is all the more important, that they continue this upward climb at an accelerated pace, if anything. It is quite a responsibility for one, when he makes this decision to serve the Father. The rewards are greater than can be imagined, but you must be steadfast in holding to this decision. Your earthly employer, will no longer seem important, as you have an even greater employer, who offers fringe benefits that are hard to conceive of. You will now mingle with the greats of your time, after you make such a decision as this. All of this may seem to be important, but you will now find that this is not important to you, as it might have been before. At this point, you will be truly free. You will be free from all the petty, negative thoughts that were important to you before. You will be free to tune in to the great souls of all time, as you will be one with them.